# Fife
## 40 Heritage & History Walks

The author and publisher have made every effort to ensure that the information in this publication is accurate, and accept no responsibility whatsoever for any loss, injury or inconvenience experienced by any person or persons whilst using this book.

*For Jim and Avril Milne who gave me my love of walking.*

published by
**pocket mountains ltd**
The Old Church, Annanside,
Moffat DG10 9HB

ISBN: 978-1-916739-12-3

Text and photography copyright © Douglas Milne 2025

The right of Douglas Milne to be identified as the Author of this work has been asserted by him in accordance with the Copyright, Designs and Patents Act 1988

A catalogue record for this book is available from the British Library

Contains Ordnance Survey data © Crown copyright and database 2025

All rights reserved. No part of this publication may be reproduced, stored in a retrieval system, or transmitted in any form or by any means, electronic or mechanical, including photocopying and recording, unless expressly permitted by Pocket Mountains Ltd.

Printed by J Thomson Colour Printers, Glasgow

# Introduction

Bounded by the Firth of Tay to the north and the Firth of Forth to the south, the Kingdom of Fife stretches out into the North Sea from Scotland's east coast. Home to one of the world's oldest universities, the former seat of Scotland's monarchy and the birthplace of golf, this historic peninsula is also a walkers' paradise. There is something for everyone here: gentle strolls in wooded nature reserves and country parks, strenuous hikes in the Lomond and Ochil Hills, and nearly 200km of rugged coastline dotted with historic ports, from the industrial docks of Burntisland and Rosyth to the quaint fishing villages of the East Neuk.

Fife is home to two of Scotland's long-distance walking trails. The Fife Coastal Path, which is the longest continuous coastal path in Scotland, follows the county's eastern perimeter from Kincardine on the Firth of Forth to Newburgh on the Firth of Tay. Meanwhile the Fife Pilgrim Way charts the route taken by pilgrims who arrived in Fife at Culross or at North Queensferry, using the ferry service set up by Queen Margaret for that purpose. Their route took them to the great abbey at Dunfermline and onwards to St Andrews.

### History
According to legend, the first king of the Picts was Cruithne, whose seven sons gave their names to the regions of Pictland. One of these Pictish regions, *Fibh*, became Fife. From medieval times, Fife was a favoured place of royalty. King Malcolm Canmore made Dunfermline his base, and the city was the capital of Scotland until the death of James I in 1437. King Malcolm's wife, Queen Margaret, founded a church for Benedictine monks, which grew into an abbey during the reign of their son, David I. The abbey is the last resting place for a total of 18 Scottish royals, including seven kings. Margaret was canonised in 1250. Near the abbey are the ruins of Dunfermline Palace, which was a royal residence until James VI and I moved his court south in 1603.

There is another royal palace in Falkland, which was favoured by the Stuarts as a place of hunting and feasting. Fife's pretensions to a kingdom did not come from the Stuarts nor any other royal dynasty, but from medieval historians such as Andrew of Wyntoun, who described Fife as 'ane Kynrick' (a kingdom) in his *Orygynale Cronykil of Scotland*, written some time after 1420.

### The natural environment
The ancient Kingdom of Fife is said to have been described by King James VI of Scotland as 'a beggar's mantle fringed wi' gold'. Fife's landscape is rich and extremely varied. Mostly relatively flat, it is nevertheless interrupted by ranges such as the Ochils, the Lomonds and the Cleish and Benarty Hills. These uplands offer distinctive skylines and expansive views,

while the lowland hills and valleys are more subtle but equally varied. The region, which covers over 1300 sq km, has 170km of coastline lined with beaches and offshore islands. The Eden, Leven and Ore Rivers run through Fife, contributing to its rich biodiversity, including Special Protection Areas, National Nature Reserves and other protected sites. Coastal terraces, cliffs and the intertidal shores further define Fife's character, with landscapes influenced by the sea, weather and natural elements.

**How to use this guide**
This guide contains 40 coastal, low-level and hill walks. All are on obvious paths or tracks, and are generally waymarked or easy to follow; however, you should not wholly rely on a smartphone to find your way. Using GPS can quickly drain your phone's battery, as can cold weather. A phone signal might not always be available. Always carry the relevant map and compass and learn how to use them. The requisite OS Explorer maps (367, 370 and 371) are noted in the text. Accidents can happen anywhere. Always let someone know where you are going and when you expect to return.

Always check the weather and dress appropriately. Wear good-quality walking boots and carry warm, waterproof clothing, even if you don't think you'll need it. Walking poles are always handy.

On coastal routes, rocks can be slippery, and waves can easily sweep you into the water. Check the tides before setting out. Read through your route carefully, and be sure that it is within the capabilities of everyone in your group.

**Public transport**
There are regular bus services to the start of many of the walks, often with a connecting bus from Edinburgh, Glasgow or Dundee via Dunfermline, Kirkcaldy, Glenrothes, Leven or Cupar. Be aware that bus routes are subject to change, so these should be checked before commencing your walk if you are relying upon a bus being available (travelinescotland.com).

Train services run between Edinburgh and Dundee with stations at North Queensferry, Inverkeithing, Dalgety Bay, Aberdour, Burntisland, Kinghorn, Kirkcaldy, Markinch, Ladybank, Springfield, Cupar and Leuchars (for St Andrews). The Fife Circle Line covers Rosyth, Dunfermline, Cowdenbeath, Lochgelly, Cardenden and Glenrothes with Thornton before returning down the main line via Markinch. A new branchline to Leven from Thornton via Cameron Bridge was opened in June 2024.

**Access**
The Land Reform (Scotland) Act of 2003 gives members of the public a right to access most Scottish land and inland waters, and landowners have a responsibility not to unreasonably

prevent or deter access. However, key to the Act is that members of the public should exercise their rights responsibly, as laid out in the Scottish Outdoor Access Code (outdooraccess-scotland.scot).

These include taking your litter home with you, respecting the environment and private property, and taking care not to damage fences and crops. Close all gates behind you. Dogs should be kept under control, particularly in the spring and early summer when they could disturb ground-nesting birds. Do not enter a field with your dog if there are lambs and calves. If you enter a field where there are animals, keep your dog on a short lead and stay as far away from the animals as possible. If cattle become aggressive, keep calm, let your dog go, and take the shortest, safest route out of the field. Please pick up after your dog.

Fife is world famous as the home of golf, and a number of the walks in this guide use core paths which pass across or near some of the Kingdom's many golf courses. You should exercise care to avoid disturbance to players and to ensure the safety of yourself and others in your party. Stick to the route and keep off the greens and tees. If a golfer is taking a shot, wait until the shot has been played. Stay alert, listening for the warning 'Fore', which means that a shot has been played nearby. Finally, always follow local warning signs and keep your dog on a lead at all times.

**The Firth of Tay** laps against Fife's northern shore. Already beginning to widen at Newburgh in the northwestern corner of Fife, by the time it reaches Wormit, where the Tay Bridge stretches across the Firth beside the remains of Thomas Bouch's ill-fated original (which collapsed into the Tay in December 1879), it is 3km wide. A little further on, its younger sibling the Tay Road Bridge carries traffic across to Dundee.

Before the bridges were built, a ferry service carried trains from Ferryport-on-Tay (now Tayport) to Broughty Ferry – the final incarnation of a service which stretched back well over a thousand years. The service was popular with pilgrims travelling from St Andrews to Arbroath Abbey, and had been appropriated by the monks of Arbroath Abbey for that purpose.

North West Fife is crossed by the northern extremity of the Ochil Hills. Smaller and more rounded than the hills at the western end of the range, the pass at Lindores is still the easiest route through them. Once a medieval way, the A91 runs along the southern foot of the Ochils all the way from Stirling. As it continues eastwards towards St Andrews, it passes through Cupar, once Fife's county town and the centre of the judiciary.

Robert II made Cupar a royal burgh in 1428, but the town's importance goes back to 1276, when Alexander III held an assembly of the three estates, the clergy, nobility and burgesses – a forerunner of the Scottish Parliament – here.

# Cupar and North Fife

1. **Scotscraig Estate** — 8
   Venture into the hills above Newport-on-Tay, returning along the banks of the Tay

2. **Tayport Heath** — 10
   Take a stroll along the dunes on the shore of the Firth of Tay

3. **Morton Lochs** — 12
   How much wildlife can you spot on this scenic short circuit around a nature reserve?

4. **Lucklaw Hill** — 14
   Head up to the summit of the easternmost hill in the Ochils

5. **St Michael's Wood** — 16
   Enjoy this quiet country walk along a former railway line and through peaceful woodland

6. **Lindores Loch loop** — 18
   Make a circuit above this nature-rich loch tucked away in the Ochils

7. **Auchtermuchty Common** — 20
   Climb gently into the Ochil Hills to explore the commonlands of the people of Auchtermuchty

8. **Birnie and Gaddon Lochs** — 22
   Walk around these two former quarries which have been transformed into a thriving nature reserve

9. **The Waterless Road to Scotstarvit** — 24
   Follow in the footsteps of pilgrims to leave Ceres and climb to a hilltop monument

# Scotscraig Estate

**Distance** 7.2km **Time** 2 hours 15
**Terrain** private roads, unsurfaced tracks; mild ascent and descent
**Map** OS Explorer 371 **Access** buses to Newport from Kirkcaldy and Dundee

**Explore an ancient wooded estate before returning along the banks of the Firth of Tay.**

Scotscraig got its name from its 13th-century owner Sir Michael Scott and was later the home of Archbishop James Sharp, who was murdered by Covenanters near St Andrews in 1679. In an arrangement which was unusual for the time, the 19th-century owners, the Maitland Dougalls, allowed free access to the estate to the people of Tayport. Following the First World War, the estate was bought by the Corporation of Dundee, which intended to use it for industrial development. Fortunately, a private owner bought the land in 1925 and it remains open to the public.

The route begins at the Tay Road Bridge South Access car park which serves as a viewpoint for the Tay Road Bridge, opened in August 1966 to replace a ferry service between Dundee and Newport-on-Tay. Keeping the Tay to your left, follow a gravel track from the corner of the car park down a set of steps to drop to the B946. Cross over and turn right to join the Fife Coastal Path. After crossing the entrance and exit of a lay-by, cross again to take the next right, signed for the Scotscraig Estate, leaving the road via a gate and climbing a beautiful winding, wooded track, known as The Serpentine.

Go straight over three crossroads before dropping gently downhill to go through a gate across the road. Turn right at the junction beyond to walk along a more formal road, crossing a bridge over the

◀ Bluebells in Scotscraig Estate

Scotscraig Burn. Immediately after a cottage on the right, turn right through a gate, following the signposted path to Causewayhead, and walk up the edge of the field beyond, swinging left at the fence at the top. Lucklaw Hill can be seen to the south.

Stay by the fence to pass a large clump of gorse bushes, going through a kissing gate to walk through the woodland beyond. Pass some ruined terraced cottages with distinctive arched windows. These were built in the 1840s to house workers of Causewayhead Farm and, despite their lack of facilities, remained occupied until the 1950s. Meeting a vehicle track, turn left, then hard right, almost doubling back to pass between Causewayhead Farm and some more cottages. These were built in the 1930s to rehouse the tenants from the old cottages.

Continue down to the end of the road, carefully crossing the busy A92 at the staggered pedestrian crossing. Turn left to drop down Station Brae into Newport, and then right down Cupar Road. At the bottom of the hill, cross Tay Street and turn right to stroll along the waterfront. Approaching the war memorial, divert left to follow an unsurfaced track which drops almost to sea level before climbing to pass a viewpoint by the Blyth Fountain, a drinking fountain decorated with griffins and stags, which was gifted to the town in 1882 by Mrs Blyth Martin, a member of a prominent Dundee jute family.

Stay on the track until it exits back onto Tay Street and continue along the road to pass beneath the Tay Road Bridge. Cross the road to follow the outward route back to the car park.

# Tayport Heath

**Distance** 6.7km **Time** 2 hours
**Terrain** sandy tracks, beach and surfaced tracks **Map** OS Explorer 371 **Access** bus to Tayport from Glenrothes, St Andrews, Kirkcaldy and Dundee. The beach section of this walk may not be passable at high tide – check tide times

Explore the eastern end of the Firth of Tay in this pleasant walk along its southern shore, returning by the Fife Coastal Path.

Tayport was originally known as Southferry, which derived from its full name of South Ferry of Portincraig, from the Gaelic *port na creige*, meaning 'harbour of the rock'. From here, a ferry ran to Northferry. The service began well before 1180, when the land here was granted to Arbroath Abbey, but it was well used by pilgrims travelling from St Andrews to Arbroath. By the 19th century, Northferry had become Broughty Ferry, while Southferry became Ferry-Port-on-Craig. After a railway ferry was established in 1851, the name was replaced with the simpler 'Tayport'.

The walk begins at the car park on Links Road North in Tayport. Go along the path which leaves the car park towards the sea, turning right onto another track. You can't miss the row of concrete blocks which were placed on the shore in 1941 to protect against invading enemy tanks during the Second World War. Since then, the shoreline has shifted seaward at a rate of five metres a year.

# TAYPORT HEATH

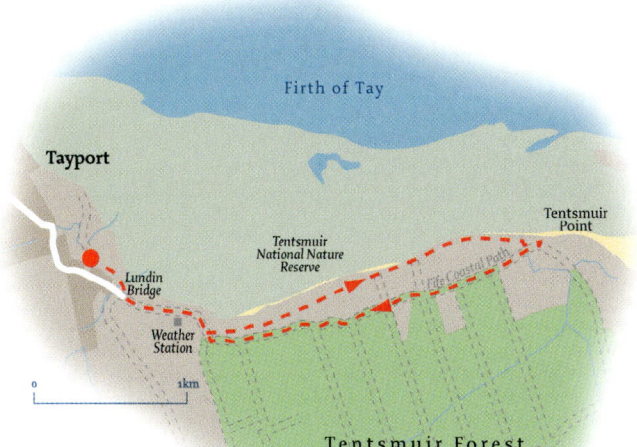

The River Tay, Scotland's longest river, discharges more water into the sea than any other river in the UK. The sheer volume of water moves sand around, and the coast here is constantly growing and retreating. Consequently, this is a valuable site for the study of coastal development and change. Eight thousand years ago, the shore was 3km further inland, near modern-day Morton Lochs.

Reaching the end of the path, turn left to cross the Lundin Burn, keeping left again to go around a gate. Continue along the single-track road before bearing right at a fork, keeping on the main path. Look out for the pair of pillboxes which can be explored to the right.

Just before the gate, bear left to walk along a sandy path across the dunes, which are clad with heather, broom and gorse. Reaching a beach after 1.2km, continue eastwards across the sand. The anti-tank defences stretch west to east across the beach. Dundee, Broughty Ferry and Monifieth can be seen across the Firth. At the far end of the beach, climb a sandy path back into the dunes. Passing a very large dune on the right, with a line of tree stumps on its top, swing inland before turning left to continue across the dunes.

Turn right, where a sign indicates the way back to Tayport, then right again to follow a surfaced vehicle track on the edge of Tentsmuir Forest – this is the route of the Fife Coastal Path and in the early 1800s it would have been on the shore.

Stay on the main track, ignoring all routes off to the left and right, to return to the beginning of the walk.

◀ Anti-tank defences by the River Tay

# Morton Lochs

**Distance** 1.6km **Time** 30 minutes
**Terrain** good surfaced paths throughout
**Map** OS Explorer 371 **Access** no public transport to the start

This short relaxing circuit along accessible pathways explores a peaceful nature reserve. In the early 20th century, this was a boggy moorland of dune heath. In 1906, the Christie family, local landowners, created three small lochs by flooding the area and stocked them with trout and other fish for private fishing.

The lochs quickly attracted wintering wildfowl and became an important freshwater habitat. They were designated as the UK's second National Nature Reserve in 1952, recognising their importance. Today, they are part of the Tentsmuir National Nature Reserve.

Excavations have found that Morton Lochs is one of the oldest occupied sites in the whole of Scotland. Around 8000 years ago, Mesolithic people arrived here. They gathered roots, seeds, nuts and fruit, and also hunted for game and fowl. The remains of haddock, turbot and cod have been found in prehistoric middens, telling us that they were expert fishermen.

As you wander around the reserve, look out for buzzards soaring over the treetops, and red squirrels in the trees and scampering across the forest floor. Red squirrels need a minimum of 200 hectares of coniferous woodland to thrive and Morton Lochs provides them with the perfect habitat. Watch out too for insects such as the common blue, comma, meadow brown and orange-tip butterflies.

The walk begins at the Morton Lochs NNR car park, at the end of an unnamed road off the B945, 2.7km south of Tayport.

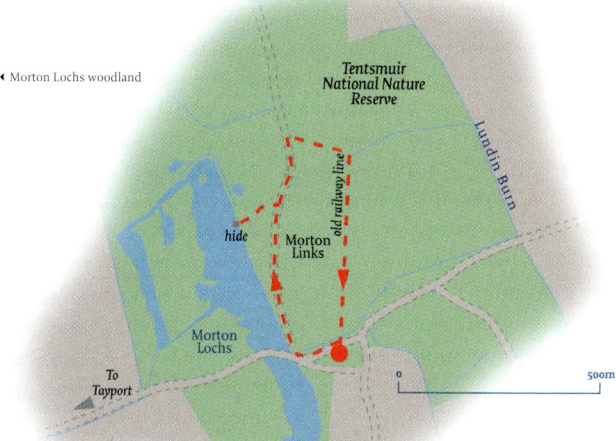

◀ Morton Lochs woodland

The car park sits beside a bridge across the former Edinburgh and Northern Railway, which closed in 1959.

Cross the road at the opposite end of the car park from the bridge. The line of the old railway stretches out straight ahead, but take a sharp left to head down a path, quickly entering woodland.

Turn right at a junction. There is a bird hide on the left here, which overlooks one of the lochs. Watch out for mute swans and in the early morning or at dusk, if you keep very quiet, you might be lucky enough to catch a glimpse of an otter.

Continue along the path, turning left through a gate to meander through the trees. A bird hide can be seen straight ahead, but detour left as you approach it to circle a pond on a little wooden walkway. Morton Lochs is an ideal habitat for dragonflies and damselflies and has been designated a dragonfly hotspot by the British Dragonfly Society. They play a vital role in wetland ecosystems, eating insects and other invertebrates and in turn providing a food source for birds and amphibians. Watch out for common hawker, common darter, black darter and the four-spotted chaser dragonflies, as well as common blue, azure, emerald, large red and blue-tailed damselflies.

Leaving the pond drop into the hide for views across the loch. From here, you can spot moorhen, little grebe, march harrier, kingfisher, teal, water rail, tufted duck, wigeon and goldeneye.

From the hide, wander back up to the gate, turning left onto the main path. Take the next right, and right again at the junction to follow the old railway line back to the car park.

# Lucklaw Hill

**Distance** 6.3km **Time** 2 hours
**Terrain** minor roads and farm tracks, forest and hill tracks; some mild ascent and descent **Map** OS Explorer 371
**Access** buses to Balmullo from Edinburgh, Kirkcaldy, St Andrews and Dundee

**Despite its diminutive size, the extensive views from the summit of Lucklaw Hill are a highlight of this pleasant circuit above the former weaving village of Balmullo. The name of the village was recorded as 'Beilmullhoh' in 1282, and is derived from the Celtic *baile mullaich*, meaning 'the top village'.**

Beginning at Burnside Hall in Balmullo, cross the playing field beside the hall, aiming for the corner on the right where a track disappears behind a line of trees. Stroll along the track to leave the village, turning left at a crosspaths to follow a vehicle track between fields.

Turn right at the end to reach Cuplahills Farm, then take a hard right through a gate at a sign for a Woodland Walk. Bear left just before another gate, then left again to climb a grassy trod into woodland. This is Willie's Wood, planted by former Cuplahills resident Willie Melville to encourage birdlife. When Willie died in 2016, his ashes were scattered in the woodland.

Head through the woods, descending to continue straight ahead where another track joins from the left. Passing the end of a drystane dyke, bear left to climb uphill through a brief gully before continuing through a tree tunnel.

Emerging onto a farm road, turn left, then right at the junction to reach a minor road. Turn immediately right here, going along a single-track road and ignoring the sign on the corner for the woodland walk.

After 500m, turn left to climb steps into Lucklaw Wood, and head up a wide track through the trees. This is another of

◀ Willie's Wood

Willie Melville's creations. Bear right at a clearing, then turn left at the end of the track to climb uphill.

Bear right to descend slightly to reach two gates. Go through the one on the right, crossing the field beyond and turning right at the fence on the far side to climb to a gate in the top corner. On the other side of the gate, go along a wide track, bearing right, then left to wind up to a prominent communications mast at the summit of Lucklaw Hill.

The summit offers superb views across the Tay to Dundee, along the Firth of Tay and round by northeast Fife, past St Andrews and down towards Fife Ness.

At 190m above sea level, Lucklaw Hill is the easternmost extremity of the Ochil Hills, which stretch from here down to Stirling. In the 1790s, it was reported that the hill was an ancient hunting ground for the kings of Scotland, but there are no records to support this.

Head past the trig point to go downhill through heather on a narrower hill track. Turn right by the corner of an old stone wall, going down the edge of a field onto a tree-lined lane and following it to the junction at the bottom of the hill.

Turn right to walk back into Balmullo and continue through the village. Turn right up Burnside, then left past some bollards to return to Burnside Hall.

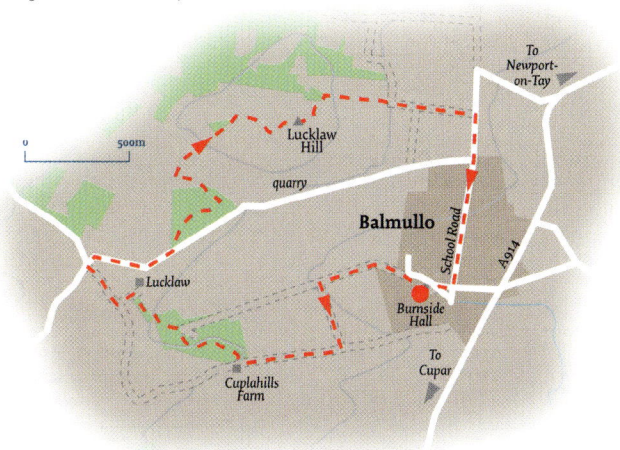

# St Michael's Wood

**Distance** 7.8km **Time** 2 hours 15 **Terrain** unsurfaced tracks, minor country roads **Map** OS Explorer 371 **Access** buses to Leuchars (School Hill) from St Andrews and Dundee; trains to Leuchars from Edinburgh, Kirkcaldy and Dundee

**Follow an old railway line, returning through quiet woodland and an historic coffin road.**

The walk begins in Leuchars at the junction of Main Street and Station Road. Go up the path beside the Commercial Arms and through a couple of gates to continue along an old railway embankment. This is the route of the Edinburgh and Northern Railway, which opened in 1848 to carry passengers from Burntisland to Ferryport-on-Craig (the original name for Tayport, a few miles north from here), where a specially designed ferry carried the train across the Tay to Broughty Ferry. Though the line was initially busy when it first opened in 1850, it became a branchline in 1878, when traffic was diverted from Leuchars to Wormit and over the newly-opened Tay Bridge, and closed in 1959.

An ornate doocot on the left once provided pigeons to Leuchars Castle. Further along, a raised mound was the site of the castle itself, which existed before 1264 but was demolished in the 19th century.

Reaching a single-track road, turn left, keeping with it as it veers right and then left. Where the road swings right again, go left to head along a farm road. At the house just before the woodland, bear right, then cross a small field to enter St Michael's Wood. Immediately go straight over a crosspaths, then turn right to continue along the main track. Head straight across a staggered crosspaths, staying on the main track to emerge onto a road.

Turn left and then left again to walk along the pavement into St Michaels.

# St Michael's Wood

◀ St Michael's Wood

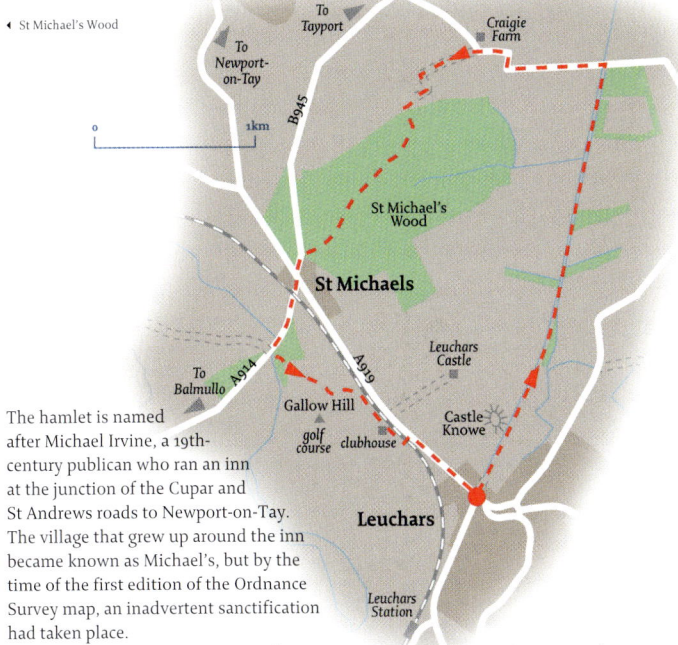

The hamlet is named after Michael Irvine, a 19th-century publican who ran an inn at the junction of the Cupar and St Andrews roads to Newport-on-Tay. The village that grew up around the inn became known as Michael's, but by the time of the first edition of the Ordnance Survey map, an inadvertent sanctification had taken place.

Turn right by St Michaels Inn, walking along the pavement beside the A914 and passing beneath a railway bridge. Further on, turn left through a stone gateway, following a sign for the coffin road, to walk along a footpath between two houses and into woodland, where a narrow track climbs through the trees to emerge onto a golf course.

As a coffin road, this would have been the route along which funeral processions carried coffins to the 12th-century St Athernase Church in Leuchars for burial. As such, the waymarked route across the golf course is a core path, but be sure to give way to golfers.

Continue straight ahead, passing a waymarker and turning left at the next one. Bear right at a junction, briefly passing through trees, and follow the waymarkers across the golf course before turning right onto an unsurfaced vehicle track which runs parallel to the railway line. Go around the gate by the clubhouse, crossing an old stone bridge over the railway and turning right to follow the A919 back into Leuchars and the beginning of the walk.

# Lindores Loch loop

**Distance** 6.5km **Time** 2 hours
**Terrain** mostly unsurfaced tracks, minor roads, one short section on a busy road with no pavement; short but steep ascents and descents **Map** OS Explorer 370
**Access** buses to Grange of Lindores from Glenrothes and Perth

**Walk around beautiful Lindores Loch, mostly on the hillsides above the loch, and only rarely touching its banks.**

The loch is nestled in the Ochil Hills, and was formed from meltwater from the hills during the last ice age. It is a shallow loch, with a maximum depth of only three metres.

The walk begins in the car park beside Abdie and Dunbog Parish Church, designed by William Burn and completed in 1827. Go along the single-track road which parallels the railway line, passing ruined Abdie Church. Named St Magradin's before the Reformation, the church was consecrated by Bishop David de Bernham in 1242. It was controlled by the monks of Lindores Abbey, just outside nearby Newburgh. When the abbey was granted a charter in 1178, Lindores Parish became Abdie, from the Gaelic for 'abbey land', *apainn*.

Immediately before the entrance to Abdie House, turn right through a gate, then immediately left to go along the edge of a paddock. Beyond another gate at the far end, turn left along the side of a field.

# Lindores Loch loop

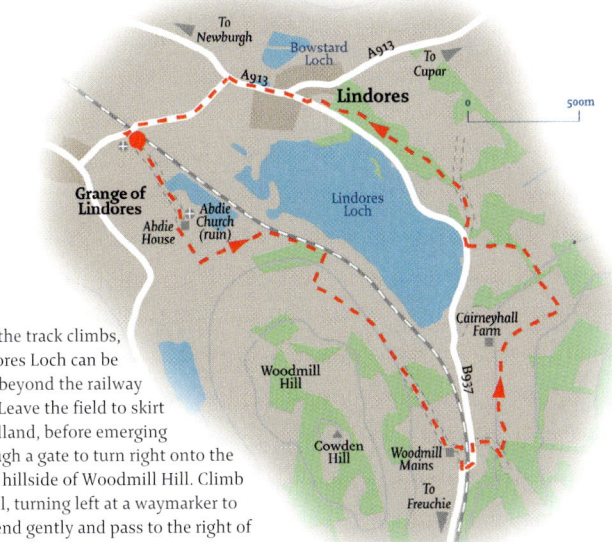

As the track climbs, Lindores Loch can be seen beyond the railway line. Leave the field to skirt woodland, before emerging through a gate to turn right onto the open hillside of Woodmill Hill. Climb uphill, turning left at a waymarker to descend gently and pass to the right of a gate. Go through another gate and continue down a wide unsurfaced vehicle track beyond.

Keep left past Woodmill Mains, turning left onto the B937, then right after 130m to climb a rough vehicle track. Take a sharp left by a waymarker to amble along the edge of woodland and through a gate.

Go along a grassy trod by a fence, bearing right to climb to a gate, going through it and continuing to another gate. Do not go through this one, but instead turn left to follow a burn downhill, turning right, then immediately left at the bottom to go through a gate. Continue down a tree-lined track, turning left onto an access road down to the B937. Go very briefly right on this, then sharp right to leave the road through stone gateposts, passing a field on the left and bearing left immediately after the field to head along a woodland track.

Bear left to emerge onto the B937, turning right to go into Lindores. The village's name derives either from the Gaelic *lann doras*, meaning 'the church at the pass', or from *linn doras*, 'the loch at the pass'. The pass in question was historically an important route through the Ochil Hills to the Tay, and is the route of the railway today.

Turn left at the junction, following the A913 out of the village, proceeding very carefully for a further 120m along the busy road after the pavement ends, before turning left along a single-track road to return to the beginning of the walk.

◀ Abdie Church

# Auchtermuchty Common

**Distance** 7.1km **Time** 2 hour 15
**Terrain** minor roads, unsurfaced paths
**Map** OS Explorer 370 **Access** buses to
Auchtermuchty from Glenrothes, Perth
and St Andrews

**Climb into the hills above Auchtermuchty to explore the grazing land granted to the town by King James V.**

Auchtermuchty is situated where the Ochil Hills rise out of the low, flat ground of the Howe of Fife. It was the location of a Roman camp in 208-210AD, when the army of Septimius Severus cut through Fife from North Queensferry to the River Tay. The town's name comes from the Pictish *uachdarmuc*, meaning 'the high ground of the wild boar'. It became a royal burgh in 1517, when it was granted a charter by James V, allowing the town to hold fairs and markets, and to charge stallholders a fee.

Begin at the junction between High Street and Cupar Road. Go along High Street, continuing straight ahead at the junction with Pitmedden Wynd before taking the third right up Leckiebank Road. Leaving the village, continue straight ahead at the entrance to Baincraig.

Turn right at a Fife Core Paths waymark along the edge of a field, going left at the end to follow a burn upstream, crossing it at a footbridge and turning right on rejoining the access road for Leckiebank.

Turn left at the road end to follow a minor road gently uphill, turning right into the Clink car park. Skirt around the gate at the far end and continue along a wide woodland track through Pitmedden Forest. Go straight over a junction, then, ignoring the first track on the right, bear right at the second to head downhill.

Turn left at the bottom, following a gravel drive downhill, then go right onto

# Auchtermuchty Common

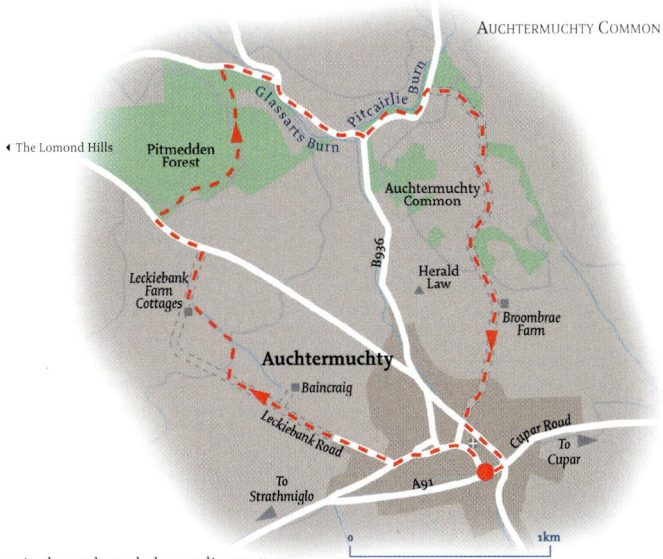

a single-track road, descending to turn right onto another road, which follows the Glassarts Burn through a gorge.

Turn left onto the B936, quickly turning left again to follow an unsurfaced track and then a wooden boardwalk along the Pitcairlie Burn. When the track rises to the road again, cross over to go through the Auchtermuchty Common car park. Dodge around the gate at the far end, and continue up an unsurfaced vehicle track across the common.

James V's charter granted a large area of grazing land to Auchtermuchty, and the town's householders continue to hold the right to graze animals, fly falcons and cut turf on the common to this day. In 1974, the Macduff Trust was set up to manage the common on behalf of the burgh. There are around 50 species of grasses and wildflowers here, including toadflax, yellow rattle, knapweed and scabious. The ground is too rough for modern machinery, so grazing ponies and sheep are used to prevent gorse, broom and other shrubs from invading. Pearl-bordered fritillary, peacock and common blue are among the 15 species of butterfly found here in summer.

The track leads between two drystane dykes, going through a couple of gates before joining an unsurfaced farm track which climbs up and over the brow of a hill, offering an excellent view of the Lomond Hills, before dropping down towards Auchtermuchty. Arriving back in the town, turn left at the bottom. Turn right at the end of the road to return to the beginning of the walk.

# Birnie and Gaddon Lochs

**Distance** 3km **Time** 1 hour
**Terrain** surfaced path throughout
**Map** OS Explorer 370 **Access** no public transport to the start

Birnie and Gaddon Lochs began as two sand and gravel quarries in the late 1980s, but as the pits deepened the quarries flooded. As a result, they were closed in the early 1990s and sold to Fife Council for £1 each. Left to return to nature, the site quickly attracted wildlife and was declared a Local Nature Reserve in 2000.

The site has been enhanced by the addition of plants such as kingcup, water mint, water forget-me-not, lesser pond sedge, elderflower and northern marsh orchid. All are native to Fife, and were collected from local ponds and lochs. The flowers attract insects and the seeds provide food for birds and mammals. Emergent plants at the water's edge provide shelter for tadpoles and allow dragonflies and damselflies to climb out of the water as they metamorphise into adults.

The walk begins in the Birnie Loch Nature Reserve car park, 500m south along the B937 from its junction with the A91. Facing the loch, take the path to the right, bearing right at a fork to cross the Collessie Burn. Follow a tree-lined surfaced path to continue anti-clockwise around the edge of Gaddon Loch.

The trees around the lochs have been chosen to provide a habitat for birds, insects, flowers and fungi, while their blossom and fruit attract wildlife. Small birds such as sand martin, goldcrest, bullfinch, dunnock and willow warbler flit amongst the branches. In the autumn, look for fungi such as brown birch bolete beneath the trees.

After rounding the southeastern end of

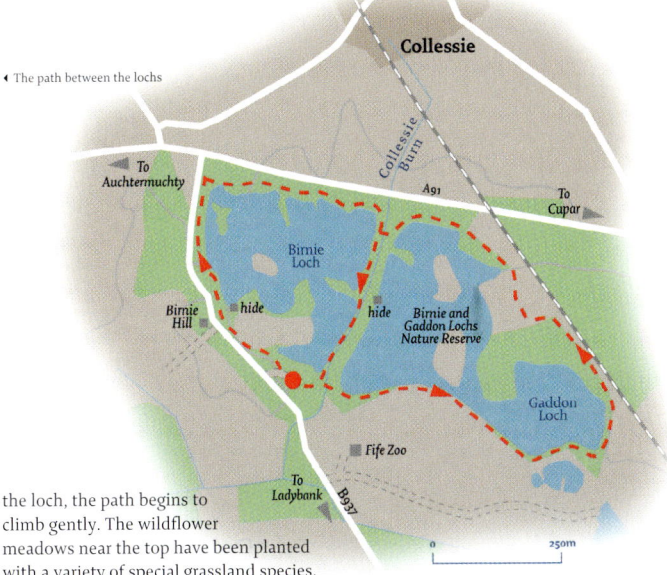

◀ The path between the lochs

the loch, the path begins to climb gently. The wildflower meadows near the top have been planted with a variety of special grassland species, which are irresistible to butterflies such as red admiral, and are of great benefit to the biodiversity of the site.

Bear left, where the views across the lochs are superb. Dropping back down to loch-level again, ruined buildings are remnants of the site's former function as a quarry. Cross a bridge over the Collessie Burn, which flows between the two lochs on a causeway. Reaching a junction, turn left to cross the causeway.

Look out for a bird hide overlooking Gaddon Loch on the left. The lochs attract large flocks of wildfowl, especially in winter. Mallard, kingfisher, mute swan, grey heron, wigeon, greylag goose, goosander, lapwing, oystercatcher and redshank can all be spotted from here.

Continue along the causeway back towards the car park. Reaching the car park, turn right to walk along the loch shore, bearing right past an information board to follow another tree-lined surfaced path around the edge of Birnie Loch. There is another bird hide on the right. The site provides food, safe roosts and nesting sites, and some birds spend their whole life here.

Cross a wooden bridge over an outlet from the loch, which allows it to overflow into the Collessie Burn, to return to the causeway and follow it back to the start.

# The Waterless Road to Scotstarvit

**Distance** 10.4km **Time** 3 hours 15
**Terrain** surfaced and unsurfaced roads and tracks; steep ascent **Map** OS Explorer 370
**Access** buses to Ceres from Kirkcaldy, St Andrews, Glenrothes and Dundee

**Follow a traditional route from Ceres before admiring the views from the summit of Hill of Tarvit.**

The walk begins at the South Croftdyke car park in the historic village of Ceres. Head up Woodburn Road, a narrow road directly opposite the entrance to the car park, which becomes an unsurfaced vehicle track as it climbs out of the village. This is the Waterless Road, a traditional route taken by pilgrims on their way to St Andrews, which now forms part of the Fife Pilgrim Way.

At the farm at Denhead, turn right, staying on the road to reach and cross the B939. Continue straight ahead down an old, very worn unsurfaced track between two drystane dykes. At the end, turn left to continue up a single-track road, passing a 17th-century doocot.

Take a hard right at the next junction, crossing Craigrothie Burn by a charming old footbridge beside a ford. At the end of the road, turn right to continue along Wemysshall Road for 250m before turning left through the gates of Hill of Tarvit to walk up the drive.

Bear left in front of the mansion house, then turn right into the car park. Cross to the diagonally opposite corner and go up an unsurfaced path which climbs steeply through woodland. Exit the trees via a stile over a wire fence. Continue up the hill on a grassy track to the monument and trig point on the summit.

# THE WATERLESS ROAD TO SCOTSTARVIT

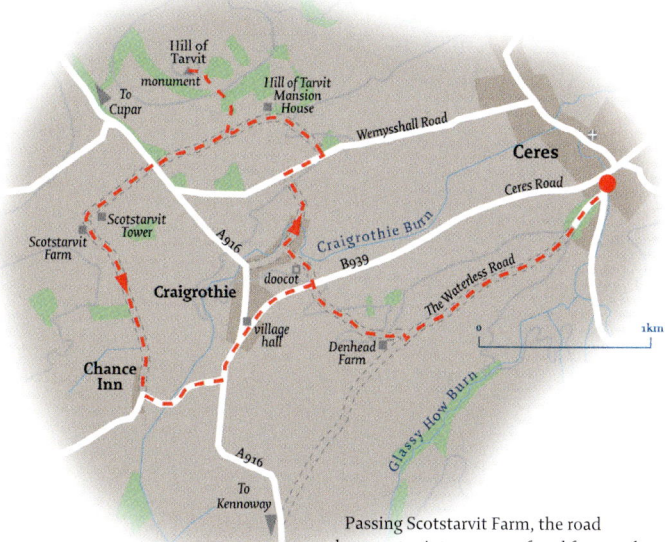

The monument was constructed in 1871 and marks the spot where the Treaty of Gairlie Bank was signed between the army of Mary of Guise, mother of Mary Queen of Scots, and the forces of the Congregation in 1559. The hill offers extensive views across this part of Fife.

Return down the hill to the car park, turning right to continue along the tree-lined western driveway. Exit through a set of gateposts, crossing the A916 to go along a farm vehicle track directly opposite, passing Scotstarvit Tower on the left. The five-storey tower was built by Sir John Scot after he purchased the Tarvit Estate in 1611, subsequently adding his own name to that of the estate, creating the name Scotstarvit.

Passing Scotstarvit Farm, the road degenerates into an unsurfaced foot track which drops down to meet the end of a road at Chance Inn. The hamlet was once a stagepost where coach horses were changed on the way to Cupar, and was originally known as Change Inn.

Continue down the road, turning left at the junction to drop out of the village and go through the countryside on a minor road. Climb to turn left onto the A916, continuing into Craigrothie on a gravel path at the side of the road. Where the village hall sits on a fork in the road, bear right along the B939. Continue carefully for a further 250m after leaving the village, where the pavement runs out, before turning right onto the road from Denhead and walking back along the outward route to return to Ceres.

◀ Monument on Hill of Tarvit

**With its quaint fishing villages** and traditional architecture, the East Neuk of Fife is one of the most picturesque parts of Scotland. Neuk is the old Scots word for a 'niche', 'nook' or 'corner', and it perfectly describes this easternmost corner of the Fife peninsula. The charming villages of Crail, Anstruther, Pittenweem, St Monans, Elie and Earlsferry were shaped by their reliance on the sea. Each has narrow streets leading down steep inclines to the sea, where red pantiled or grey slated houses with Dutch style, crow-stepped gables line picture-perfect harbours.

The buildings are a legacy of the East Neuk's trade with the Low Countries. Pantiles began to be imported from Rotterdam in the last quarter of the 17th century. They were better suited than thatch for the exposed buildings of the East Neuk, and building up the crow-stepped gable wall above the pantiles further protected them from the wind.

The bones of St Andrew, the first of Christ's apostles, were brought to Scotland after their custodian, St Rule (or Regulus), a monk or bishop from Patras in Greece, received a 'divine revelation' from the apostle in 345AD instructing him to sail to the edge of the world and build a church dedicated to St Andrew where his ship landed. Thus the Pictish settlement of Kilrymont became the Christian St Andrews. The tower of an 11th-century church dedicated to St Rule served as a landmark for pilgrims over the next few centuries, and still stands in the grounds of the now ruined medieval cathedral.

The story of St Rule's choice of Scotland gained political importance in the middle ages, when it was used by Scottish kings, nobles and churchmen to separate Scotland's identity from that of England by giving the country its own patron saint.

# St Andrews and the East Neuk

**1** **Craigtoun Country Park and Den** 28
Leave the former Mount Melville Estate to follow two wooded glens to the outskirts of St Andrews

**2** **The Rock and Spindle** 30
Take the Fife Coastal Path out of St Andrews to discover an unusual geological landmark

**3** **Kittock's Den and Buddo Rock** 32
Traverse a wooded ravine to follow the Fife Coastal Path to an impressive sea stack

**4** **Kingsbarns and Cambo** 34
Traverse the dunes beside an extensive sandy beach before returning through peaceful woodland

**5** **Crail and Fife Ness** 36
An enjoyable ramble around Fife's easternmost point

**6** **Elie and Kilconquhar Loch** 38
Head inland past a pretty loch before making your way back along the Fife Coastal Path

**7** **St Monans and Pittenweem** 40
Explore two of the East Neuk's most picturesque villages before returning via an historic estate

# 1 ST ANDREWS AND THE EAST NEUK

# Craigtoun Country Park and Den

**Distance** 6km **Time** 2 hours
**Terrain** surfaced paths, unsurfaced tracks; some mild ascent and descent
**Map** OS Explorer 371 **Access** buses to Craigtoun Country Park from Glenrothes and St Andrews

**Traverse two beautiful wooded glens before returning to the more formal setting of Craigtoun Country Park.**

The Mount Melville Estate was first established for General George Melville in 1698 and it stayed in the Melville family until 1900, when it was purchased by Dr James Younger of the Younger brewing family. Younger commissioned Paul Waterhouse to build a new mansion house and to landscape the grounds. The estate was sold to Fife County Council in 1947.

Beginning in Craigtoun's car park, go through the entrance into the park, turning right beyond a small bridge, and head towards the boating lake. This is one of two lakes added by Waterhouse in 1920 to comply with insurance company requirements for a ready water supply in case of fire. He also added the picturesque island village, known as the Dutch Village due to its white harling and red pantiled roofs. Today, a miniature railway encircles the lake.

Cross the railway track and pass the station, swinging left to cross the railway again. Go straight over a crosspaths, passing between two stone pillars and bearing right. Walk halfway around a putting green, exiting at the far side and following the sign for St Andrews. Cross a minor road and continue down a surfaced track through Craigtoun Den, following the Lumbo Burn. Keep an eye out for red squirrels among the branches or on the woodland floor.

The track descends through woodland, crossing a road and continuing straight

# CRAIGTOUN COUNTRY PARK AND DEN

◀ The Dutch Village

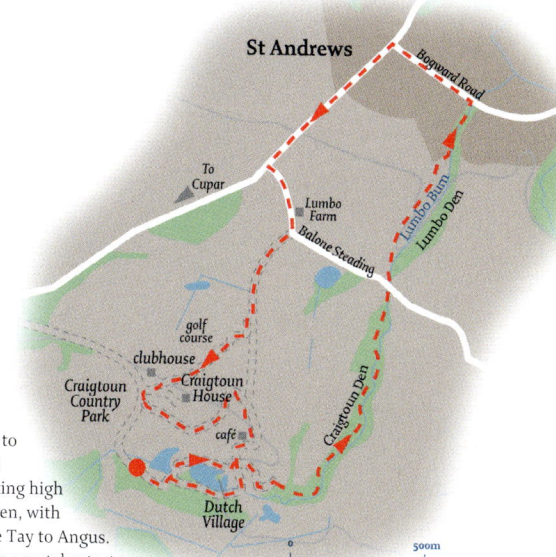

ahead. Bear left to climb out of the woodland, walking high above Lumbo Den, with views across the Tay to Angus.

Going through a metal gate, turn abruptly left to pass between a wall and the burn. Pass the ends of a couple of streets before turning left onto Bogward Road. Turn left again at the roundabout at the end of the road and continue along the pavement into the countryside.

Turn left onto Balone Steading, signed for Mount Melville. Bear right at a fork to follow a single-track road towards Mount Melville, but turn right at the next gateway to follow a surfaced path around Duke's Golf Course. Opened in 1995, The Duke's has a worldwide reputation as a heathland championship golf course.

Bear left at a fork to climb steeply but briefly uphill, keeping left again at the next fork. Younger's old mansion is on the left. This B-listed building was used as a maternity hospital until its closure in 1992.

Bear right past the clubhouse and pass the entrance to the mansion, then turn left to briefly join the entrance road to Craigtoun. Turn left through a gate, then left at a crosspaths immediately afterwards to stride along a wide aggregate surfaced path through the park.

Bear left at another fork, circling around the Italian Garden. Beyond a wishing well, keep right to pass a café, turning left at the junction and going straight over a crosspaths and across the railway line again, circling around the southern end of the lake to return to the car park.

# The Rock and Spindle

**Distance** 6.8km **Time** 2 hours
**Terrain** undulating coastal tracks, surfaced roads, unsurfaced track; some ascent and descent **Map** OS Explorer 371
**Access** buses to St Andrews from Dundee, Edinburgh, Glenrothes and Kirkcaldy

Follow the Fife Coastal Path from St Andrews to visit a pair of impressive sea stacks. Be aware that the sea stacks and a short section of the route are inaccessible at high tide.

The walk begins at St Andrews' East Sands car park. Keeping the sea on the left, walk along the path by the shore, which begins to climb as it leaves the town, quickly passing the caravans of the St Andrews Holiday Park.

At a fork by a Fife Coastal Path waymarker, bear downhill to the left, going down an unsurfaced track and a set of rough stone steps to reach a huge sea stack known as Maiden's Rock. The stack was carved out from sandstone by waves around 6500 years ago, but now lies well above the sea.

Return to the Fife Coastal Path waymarker, this time taking the other fork to climb up stone steps, ignoring the path that joins from the right. These are the Kinkell Braes, from the Gaelic *ceann coille*, meaning 'head of the wood'.

Pass the Castle Golf Course on the right. Drop down more stone steps, crossing a stile halfway down, and descend to cross the top of a small sandy bay.

Climbing away from the bay, hop across stepping stones over a boggy patch, before rounding a headland. Bear left at a fork, where the column of the Rock and

◀ The Rock and Spindle

Spindle can be seen straight ahead. While it is tempting to clamber down to the beach from here, continue along the path, climbing to a gate and descending to another before dropping down to the beach right beside the sea stack.

The Rock and Spindle is so called because of its resemblance to tools once used to spin wool and flax. By the 1740s, rocks and spindles had been replaced by spinning wheels. The 'Spindle' even has spokes, formed from basalt columns. It was formed when groundwater was boiled by molten lava, creating vents which the lava subsequently rose through.

Retrace your steps through the two gates to return to the fork, turning left to head up the hill. Go through a gate to enter the Castle Golf Course, heading up a surfaced path.

Turn right and then right again onto a single-track road to continue down to a car park by the clubhouse. Cut straight across to go up the course's entrance drive. Around 100m before arriving at the main gate and the junction with the A917, turn right to follow a narrow surfaced road across rough grass, which runs parallel to the main road.

Keep ahead towards the terraced farm cottages at Brownhills and then bear right back towards the coast. Continue downhill between the golf course and the holiday park, turning left at the end of the path to follow the outward route back to St Andrews.

# Kittock's Den and Buddo Rock

**Distance** 4.8km **Time** 1 hour 30
**Terrain** surfaced and unsurfaced tracks, damp underfoot in places; mild ascent and descent **Map** OS Explorer 371
**Access** buses to Boarhills from St Andrews and Leven

**Descend through a secluded wooded glen before following the Fife Coastal Path to an impressive sea stack.**

The name of Kittock's Den is derived from the old Scots for a mistress or a woman of 'low character', but the connection with this leafy glen which drops gently down to the sea has been lost over the years.

The walk begins in a parking lay-by by the village noticeboard in the centre of Boarhills. The village was originally named Byrehills but transitioned to Boarhills around 1817. Head along the road, climbing uphill and out of the village, then bear left by a beautifully restored 17th-century doocot, following a sign for the Fife Coastal Path.

The road quickly becomes an unsurfaced farm track running between two fields. Where a sign directs walkers on the Fife Coastal Path to the right, go straight ahead over a crossroads to continue along a grassy vehicle track which travels in a direct line on an embankment between two fields.

Turn left onto a surfaced path on the edge of Kittocks Golf Course, taking the next right to pass the fifth tee and staying alert for stray golf balls. Bear left by a kiosk to descend between well-manicured gorse hedges.

Turn right just before the path crosses a bridge over a burn, where a damp grassy track leads along the side of the burn. This is Kittock's Den, a deep wooded ravine which cuts through the golf course

# KITTOCK'S DEN AND BUDDO ROCK

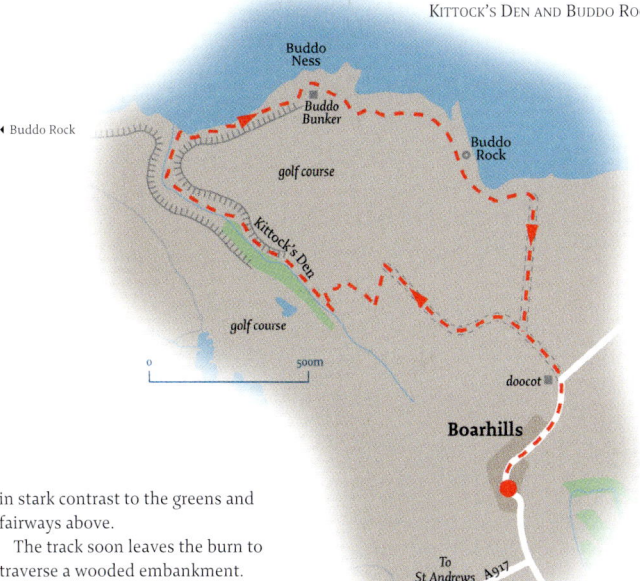

◀ Buddo Rock

in stark contrast to the greens and fairways above.

The track soon leaves the burn to traverse a wooded embankment. Continue down the hill for 800m, soon walking parallel to an old stone wall.

Reaching the bottom of the den, ignore the bridge across the burn to emerge beside the sea, turning right to head along the Fife Coastal Path, which undulates along the coast, sometimes dropping down almost to beach level and other times climbing high above the water. Although the path is well-maintained, often with stone steps to take you up and down the slopes, take care as it can be quite rough in places.

Rounding Buddo Ness, watch out on the right for a pair of well-camouflaged Second World War pillboxes, which are connected internally by a rock-cut tunnel.

Going through a gate, or over the stile beside it if it is locked, the path begins to level out. Rounding a corner, you are faced with the huge bulk of Buddo Rock, a weathered sandstone sea stack with a strange semi-detached pillar on its north side. Buddo is a local surname, and it is likely that the rock and Buddo Ness have been named after a member of this family. Once past the Rock, follow the wide well-worn path around the bay and head up the hill at the far end. Climb a stile by a gate at the top to follow a raised embankment between two fields.

Reaching a junction, turn left and follow the outward route back to the beginning of the walk.

# Kingsbarns and Cambo

**Distance** 5.4km **Time** 1 hour 45
**Terrain** unsurfaced paths, woodland tracks, minor roads; some mild ascent
**Map** OS Explorer 371 **Access** buses to Kingsbarns from Leven and St Andrews

**Kingsbarns Beach, also known as Cambo Sands, is a 3km stretch of sandy beach backed by extensive sand dunes. This walk follows the coast before climbing through the Cambo Estate.**

The route begins at Kingsbarns Beach car park (parking charge). Keeping the sea on the left, leave the car park to follow the Fife Coastal Path along the dunes.

These sand dunes, which provide food and cover for insects and small birds, help to stabilise the beach and prevent coastal erosion. Watch out for gulls, eider ducks, oystercatchers and redshanks, which feed on worms and molluscs on the beach.

Cross a wooden bridge and pass Kingsbarns Golf Links. Although the present course opened in 2000, golf has been played here since 1793. The course is ranked as one of the world's top 100 golf courses.

Continue straight on at a fork, then left by some woodland. Pass a toilet block before going through a gate on the right to enter the woodland of the Cambo Estate. Bear right to walk alongside Cambo Burn, crossing it at the next bridge on the left and turning right towards Cambo Gardens (signed).

The estate has been in the Erskine family since 1668, except for a brief period in the late 18th century when it was owned by Francis Charteris, later the 7th Earl of Wemyss. Today, Cambo is the world famous home of the Plant Heritage national collection of snowdrops, with more than 200 varieties alongside the thousands of *galanthus nivalis* which grow

◀ Kingsbarns Beach

wild in the woodlands. There is a charge should you want to enter Cambo's stunning Georgian walled garden, which dates from the 1800s.

Make your way around the side of the walled garden and stables (with excellent gift shop and café), then turn left towards the main car park. Before reaching the road, however, bear left to follow an enchanting woodland track along the Cambo Burn. The track is dotted with charming fairy buildings with tiny doors and windows attached to the trees. Climbing back towards the road, keep left to drop back to the burn.

Passing a bridge on the left, continue straight ahead, following a sign for Kingsbarns and keeping right at the next junction to climb to the road. Cross over, bearing immediately left along the woodland path on the other side.

Swing right by the estate's entrance to walk parallel to a wall, going through a small gate to continue along a wider vehicle track. At the entrance to Cambo Farm, turn left, then right to bypass a pond, bearing left beyond it to reach and cross the entrance to Kingsbarns Golf Links, continuing along the path on the other side.

Swing right, then turn sharply left by the corner of a wall, walking parallel to the wall to reach and cross another road. Approaching an open gateway in a stone wall, turn right to continue through the woodland, crossing another entrance to the golf club and going through the trees. Bear left at a fork to exit onto a road and turn right to follow it back to the Kingsbarns Beach car park.

# Crail and Fife Ness

**Distance** 10.8km **Time** 3 hours 15 **Terrain** surfaced and unsurfaced paths, beach, farm tracks **Map** OS Explorer 371 **Access** buses to Crail (Bowling Green Place) from Leven and St Andrews

**This route hugs the coastline around the easternmost corner of Fife, rarely straying far from the water's edge. Some sections may not be passable at high tide – check tide times.**

Crail, from the Pictish *cair al*, for 'cliff fort', is a very old settlement. Countess Ada de Warren, mother of Malcolm IV and William I, lived here in the 1160s and William I made Crail a royal burgh in 1178.

Beginning at the junction of Marketgate and High Street, walk along High Street and then Westgate, turning left through a gap between the houses opposite Lamont Terrace. Go down the steep cobbled path, turning left at the harbour. The east pier dates from 1610, while the west pier was rebuilt in 1828 by Robert Stevenson.

Bear left up Shoregate. At the corner, climb the steps straight ahead, keeping right at the top along Castle Walk. Carry straight on along the road at the end of Castle Walk, keeping straight ahead where it joins Nethergate. Turn right down a narrow path opposite the far end of the parking spaces, which follows a lade down to the shore.

Go left at the bottom to stroll along the Coastal Path, turning hard right at a junction by the Crail Priory Doocot. As the path swings to the left, turn right to climb steps, going through a gateway and along the path beyond.

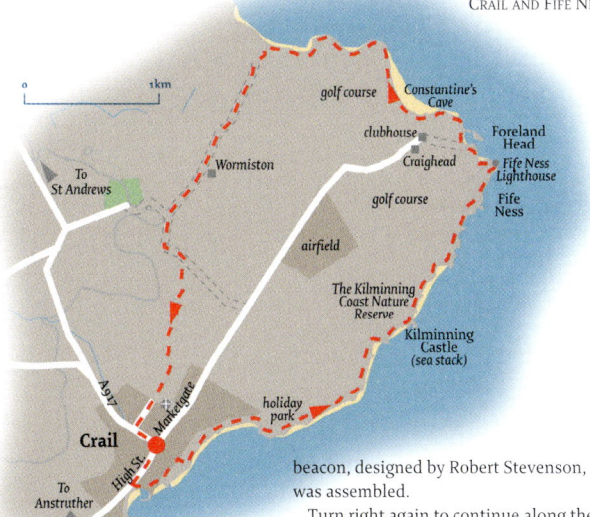

Bear right into the Pinkerton Triangle Community Wildlife Area, going through another gateway and dropping to pass through the Sauchope Links Holiday Park. At the far end, turn right, following the Fife Coastal Path sign to head across the top of a rocky bay and through a gate into the Kilminning Coast Nature Reserve.

Pass a large sea stack called Kilminning Castle and, after another gate, continue along the Coastal Path, climbing to reach the corner of a golf course before dropping to sea level again to pass the Crail Airfield Pillbox, which sits below the lighthouse on the corner of Fife Ness.

Turn right onto a road, passing Fife Ness Harbour. The harbour dates from 1537, though it is now ruined. Circles carved in the rocks show where a light beacon, designed by Robert Stevenson, was assembled.

Turn right again to continue along the edge of the golf course, following the white markers. The path soon becomes surfaced and passes Constantine's Cave, where legend says that Constantine I was killed by Vikings in 877AD. Just beyond the cave, bear right, following the white markers, and drop down to walk along the beach, before following the white markers along the edge of the golf course.

Just before a gate blocks the way, turn left to follow a fence uphill, joining a farm track. Follow the track past the farm at Wormiston, then bear left around a gate at the next corner. Turn right, then left at the next two junctions, before bearing right at a fork to pass the outskirts of Crail.

Skirt around a metal barrier to join Bow Butts Road. At the end of the road, turn left to return to the beginning of the walk.

◀ Crail Harbour

# Elie and Kilconquhar Loch

**Distance** 14.1km **Time** 4 hours
**Terrain** surfaced tracks and roads, unsurfaced woodland and coastal tracks; some steep ascent and descent
**Map** OS Explorer 371 **Access** buses to Elie (Wadeslea) from Edinburgh, Leven and St Andrews

**This superb circuit leaves Elie to pass an inland loch before returning to walk along the Fife Coastal Path.**

Beginning at the end of Elie's Admiralty Lane, by the entrance to Ruby Bay's second car park area, carry straight on along a surfaced path. Turn left at a Fife Coastal Path waymarker, then right to explore Lady's Tower. The tower was built in 1770 for Lady Janet Anstruther, who enjoyed swimming in the waters here. To ensure her privacy, whenever she fancied a swim, a servant would ring a bell in Elie to warn the residents.

Leaving the tower, turn left, bearing left again to reach Elie Ness Lighthouse, built in 1908 by David Stevenson of the Stevenson engineering dynasty.

Returning from the lighthouse, keep straight ahead up the path, turning left to pass the car park and follow Admiralty Lane to its end. Turn right onto Wadeslea, then right again to walk along the A917. Turn left through stone gateposts 100m later and continue down the long driveway of Elie House. Bear right, going around a gate and continuing straight ahead at the next two junctions.

Cross a cattle grid. Kilconquhar Loch can be seen through the trees to the right, though the view is clearer a little further on where the road passes a boathouse. Continue through ornate gates, crossing a road to go along a woodland track opposite. Exiting from the trees, turn left along a road, crossing the A917 at the junction and continuing down the road to the Elie Holiday Park.

◂ Inside Lady's Tower

Bear left at a fork, turning immediately right to continue along a wide woodland track. Go over a crosspaths, passing around the northern perimeter of the holiday park, and continue through another junction to follow the track along the peninsula of Ruddons Point, which is a Site of Special Scientific Interest.

Loop around Ruddons Point and head inland again, turning right to walk along the road through the holiday park. Where the road swings sharply to the left, bear right to follow the Fife Coastal Path over a bridge and along the shore.

Climbing a steep set of steps further on, look down to see the Elie Chain Walk below. Pass some old war defences before climbing to the trig point at the summit of Kincraig Hill. Continue past an old gun post, with excellent views across Elie and Earlsferry, before dropping steeply down to the bottom of the hill.

Bear left along a sandy path on the perimeter of Elie Golf Course, turning sharply inland at a Fife Coastal Path waymarker to cross the golf course, continuing straight ahead to walk down Chapel Green Road. Continue along Earlsferry High Street, Williamsburgh, Liberty, Links Place, Bank Street and Elie High Street, bearing right at the fork at the top of Rankeillor Street and turning right onto Stenton Row.

Keep left above Elie Harbour, then turn left up the narrow entrance to Admiralty Lane, before going right to follow the outward route back to the start.

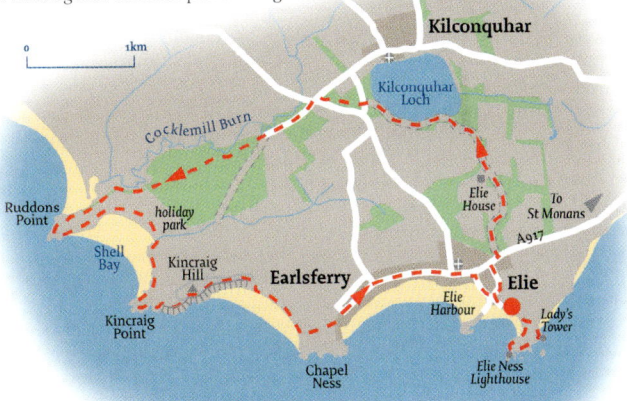

# St Monans and Pittenweem

**Distance** 9.1km **Time** 2 hours 30
**Terrain** unsurfaced tracks, roads; some steep ascent **Map** OS Explorer 371
**Access** buses to St Monans from Edinburgh, Leven and St Andrews

**Follow the Fife Coastal Path between two of the East Neuk's most sublime villages, before heading inland to return via an historic estate.**

Like all of the villages of the East Neuk, St Monans was dependent on fishing for its prosperity. In the 1860s and 1870s, the village's fishermen personally raised the finance to make improvements to the 16th-century harbour.

Pick up the Fife Coastal Path, which leaves from the far end of the car park at the end of Rose Street, passing beneath an 18th-century windmill. This was operated by the Newark Coal and Salt Company, established in 1771 by local laird Sir John Anstruther and his business partner Robert Fall. The windmill provided power to pump seawater into saltpans, which were housed in nine buildings on the raised beach below.

The Fife Coastal Path undulates along the shore. Approaching Pittenweem, bear left to climb to the West Braes viewpoint overlooking the tidal pool. Dodge behind a shelter here, continuing down to the West Shore and along the seafront, passing the brightly-painted red-tiled houses that line the coast.

Continue past the harbour, turning left through a narrow close between numbers 10 and 11 East Shore to climb steeply up several sets of steps. A caged doorway, marked with a cross, is the entrance to St Fillan's Cave. Pittenweem's name is derived from the Pictish *pett*, meaning 'place', and the Gaelic *na h-Uaimh*, 'of the cave', and this is the cave in question. It

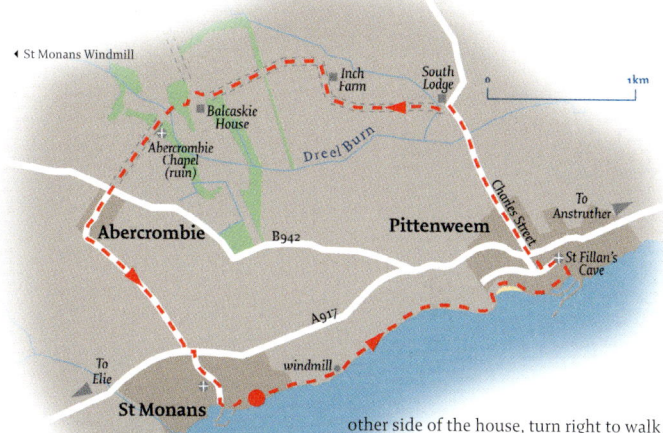

was used as a chapel by St Fillan in the 8th century.

Turn left at the top to walk down High Street, turning right up the pend of Browns Close and crossing Backgate to go up Charles Street. Cross over James Street to follow Charles Street out of the village, continuing for 800m before bearing left where the road forks, following a minor hedge-lined country road.

Continue along the road, passing between ornate gateposts and following a tree-lined driveway towards Balcaskie House, built by Sir William Bruce in 1668-74. Bruce went on to rebuild Holyrood Palace in Edinburgh for Charles II.

Bear right just before reaching the house to bypass it, going straight over a crossroads. Approaching gates at the other side of the house, turn right to walk down a woodland track, going through a gate and across a field.

Cross a bridge and over a field beyond, going through another gate and climbing through woodland. Go over a crosspaths to pass the haunting ruins of Abercrombie Chapel. It was consecrated by Bishop David de Bernham in 1247, but was abandoned in 1646 when the congregation moved to St Monans.

Pass through a gate and continue between fields to cross the B942 and go down the road opposite, heading straight through the small village of Abercrombie and onwards to arrive back at St Monans.

Cross the A917, turning left, then immediately right to walk all the way down Station Road to the harbour. Turn left along Mid Shore, bearing left to climb the hill, then right to follow Rose Street back to the beginning of the walk.

East Lomond from West Lomond ▶

**Due to their importance** for recreation and conservation, the 65 sq km of moorland, lochs and farmland of the Lomond Hills became Scotland's first regional park in 1986.

The name of this hill range is thought to be derived from a Pictish word similar to the Welsh *llumon*, meaning a 'beacon' or 'fire'. The name is apposite: a beacon lit on the hills to convey warnings or other messages would be visible from Lothian, Perthshire and Angus, and as far west as Stirling Castle, from where the similarly named Ben Lomond can be seen. While Ben Lomond rises above Loch Lomond, source of the River Leven, the Lomond Hills rise above Loch Leven, known to the Picts as *Lummonu*. The first recorded name of the hills, from 1315, was Lomondys.

The Pictish Kingdom of Fibh, from where Fife derives its name, was centred on the Lomond Hills, where two great hillforts were built on East and West Lomond. It was only in the 19th century that these two hills were given separate names – in the early 17th century, they were simply known as Lomond Hill.

In Gaelic tradition they were known as *Cuspairean Wallace* – Wallace's Goalposts – because, according to legend, William Wallace threw a putting-stone from the top of one hill to the other.

# The Lomond Hills

1. **West Lomond** — 44
   Climb to Fife's highest point for spectacular views of the Kingdom

2. **East Lomond hillfort** — 46
   Discover the site of an ancient Pictish hillfort on this short hike up Falkland Hill

3. **The Bishop** — 48
   A steep climb is rewarded with superb views over Loch Leven

4. **The Lomond Reservoirs** — 50
   Circumnavigate three wildlife-rich reservoirs nestled in the Lomond Hills Regional Park

5. **Formonthills** — 52
   Explore a scenic country park with a community woodland on the edge of Glenrothes

# West Lomond

**Distance** 8km **Time** 2 hours 30
**Terrain** hill tracks, minor road
**Map** OS Explorer 370 **Access** no public transport to the start

West Lomond is not only the highest peak in the Lomond Hills, it is also the highest point in Fife. This stunning walk climbs to the summit, returning above Harperleas Reservoir. Much of this route crosses heather moorland which is managed for red grouse, and dogs should be kept under strict control. Look out too for roe deer and foxes.

Take the track signed for West Lomond from the northwest corner of Craigmead car park, on the road between Leslie and Falkland. Turn left beyond a gate and go along a grassy track, joining a stone-surfaced track and continuing across Balharvie Moss towards West Lomond, which is unmistakable on the horizon.

Continue along the track, climbing gradually and passing through a gate, where there are excellent views back towards East Lomond. Though little is visible today, a great deal of evidence of human activity has been found along this track, including the remains of prehistoric hut circles.

Push on along the track to reach the foot of the cone-shaped summit, the remains of a volcanic plug. While it is tempting to continue straight ahead at a crosspaths to climb directly up the hill, a less strenuous option is to turn right to

# WEST LOMOND

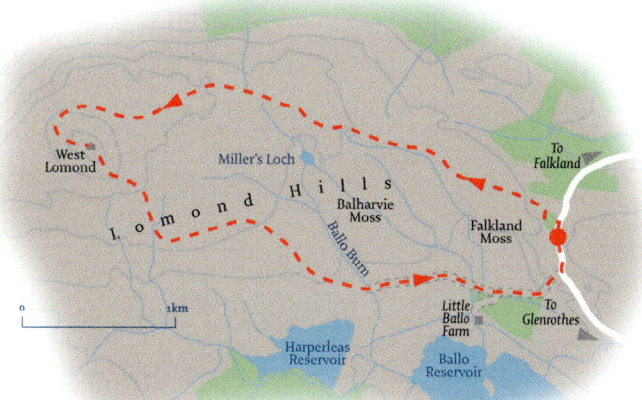

curl around the northern side of the hill.

Bear left where a narrow foot track forks off, climbing steeply up a wide grassy trod to the summit, where a trig point is surrounded by a large cairn and five circles laid out in stones. The cairn was probably constructed between the Neolithic and Bronze Age periods. When it was excavated in 1857, bones and fragments of a prehistoric cremation urn were found. The circles are thought to be the remains of post-medieval shielings.

The views are spectacular; East Lomond sits to the east, the Lomond reservoirs are laid out below to the southeast and Bishop Hill, with Loch Leven beyond, sits to the southwest. The Firth of Forth sweeps around to Edinburgh in the distant south, while the Ochil Hills line the horizon to the north.

Several tracks lead off from the summit; take the one that leads in a southeasterly direction, with Bishop Hill and Loch Leven to the right and East Lomond to the left. The track drops down before continuing straight over a crosspaths to cross a flat heather-clad plateau.

Go over a stile, before descending to a gate on the right. Do not go through the gate; instead turn left to walk across the field, descending gently to a gate in the bottom corner. Continue through a series of fields and gates until the route becomes a surfaced vehicle track.

The ruined buildings on the right are the remains of Easter Ballo Farmstead. In the mid-19th century, this was a substantial two-storey building, owned and occupied by a Major Wilson.

Continue along the vehicle track, staying on the main track at the entrance to Little Ballo. On reaching a junction with a minor country road, turn left and carry on back down to Craigmead car park.

◀ Summit of West Lomond

# East Lomond hillfort

**Distance** 3.2km **Time** 1 hour
**Terrain** hill tracks, surfaced path
**Map** OS Explorer 370 **Access** no public transport to the start

**Take this short hike to the summit of East Lomond Hill, where an impressive Iron Age hillfort once stood.**

East Lomond looms impressively over Falkland, and is known locally as Falkland Hill. The terrain is covered in wild heather moorland and is home to Fife's only population of red grouse. Dogs should be kept strictly under control.

The walk begins in the East Lomond car park at the end of a steep single-track road, signposted from the A912, 2km southeast of Falkland. The car park is free for two hours – long enough to complete this short circuit.

A well-defined unsurfaced track, signed for the East Lomond summit, leads off from the car park towards the hill. It passes through a gap in the fence, before following another fence uphill and through a gate.

Beyond the gate, stay on the main track, veering to the right as you approach the distinctive rounded summit to climb diagonally up the hillside before circling around to reach a viewing indicator at the top of East Lomond.

There are superb panoramic views from here, with the Firth of Tay to the north and the Firth of Forth to the south. Closer to hand, the Harperleas, Ballo and Holl Reservoirs can be seen to the southwest, while picturesque Falkland village is at the northeastern foot of the hill.

Established during the Iron Age, this was the site of the main fortress of the Venicones, a Celtic tribe whose name means 'the hunting hounds'. Following the fall of the Roman Empire around

◀ East Lomond summit

410AD, it became the main fortress of the Pictish Kingdom of Fibh, which gave Fife its name. The hillfort fell into disuse during the early medieval period. As well as being a royal stronghold, it was a centre for trade and craftsmanship, and was used as a refuge during times of war.

To the northwest, the Tyndall-Bruce Monument sits on Blackhill. The monument was built by Margaret Tyndall-Bruce in 1855 in honour of her husband, Onesiphorus Tyndall-Bruce, who had died that year. Through his marriage to Margaret, Tyndall-Bruce was hereditary keeper of Falkland Palace.

Continue straight across the summit and down the track on the other side, which drops steeply down the hill before levelling out to descend gently, parallel to a drystane dyke.

After a brief final drop, turn left through a gate, keeping left on the other side where an aggregate-surfaced path leads off across the hillside between two drystane dykes. Unused today, this was an original road across the Lomond Hills and is a continuation of the road which leads up to the car park from the base of the A912.

Look out, on the right, for a well-preserved early 19th-century limekiln. Dating from around 1825, it is built into raised ground, which allowed carts to load limestone into the kiln from above. After burning, the resulting lime was collected from the archways at the base of the kiln for use in agriculture and in the manufacture of lime mortar.

Follow the road back to the car park.

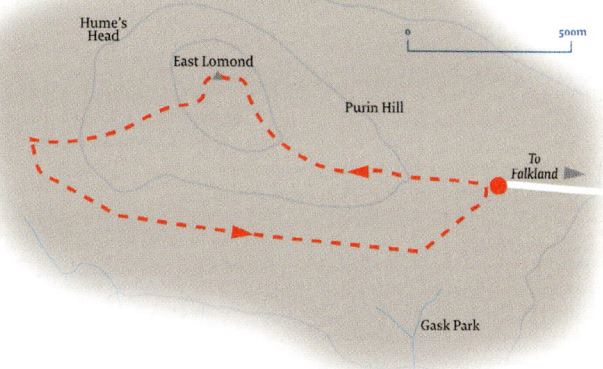

# The Bishop

**Distance** 6.8km **Time** 2 hours 30
**Terrain** hill tracks; steep ascent and descent **Map** OS Explorer 370
**Access** buses to Scotlandwell from Glenrothes and Kinross

From the 12th century, all of the land in this area was owned by the Bishopric of St Andrews, which gave its name to Bishop Hill, or as it is known locally, The Bishop. The most westerly, and probably the least popular of the Lomond Hills, it rises steeply from the eastern shore of Loch Leven to a plateau on top. The initial climb up The Bishop's steep southern scarp is a struggle, but persevere for the rewarding views across Loch Leven to the Ochil Hills, the Cleish Hills and Benarty Hill.

Look out for gliders from the Scottish Gliding Centre at Portmoak riding the thermals above the hill, along with buzzards hunting for prey. In the summer, watch out for butterflies and moths such as burnet moths, green hairstreaks, small and large whites, small blues, tortoiseshells, coppers and large skippers.

The walk begins in the car park at Portmoak Church, on the A911 north of Scotlandwell. While walkers are welcome to use the car park, they should be respectful of parking instructions, particularly on a Sunday before 11:30am.

From the car park, turn right onto the main road, turning left after 130m to climb steps and then a steep path uphill into Kilmagad Wood. This woodland has been here since at least the 1500s, when 'Wood of Kilmagade' was granted to Robert Douglas of Loch Leven. Look out for roe deer and red squirrel among the trees.

Bear right, following a sign towards

# THE BISHOP

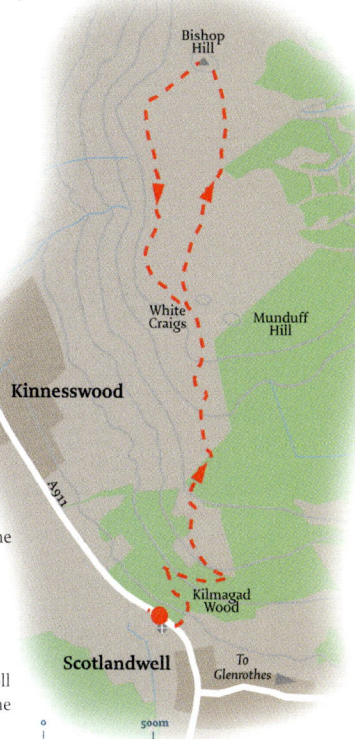

◀ Approaching The Bishop

Glenvale and climbing out of the woods, doubling back to ease the steep ascent. Stay on the main path, swinging left to go through a gate and continuing up the hill.

Passing a deep man-made channel, bear left to leave the main track, then right to follow a narrow hill track. Munduff Hill weather station dominates the hilltop to the right.

Go straight over a crosspaths to reach the flat treeless plateau at the top of the hill. Turn left to continue along a wider track. Go through a gate and another immediately to the right, then left to cross the undulating plateau towards the summit, which can be seen on a large knoll straight ahead. Cross a stile over a drystane dyke at the foot of the knoll to make the final push up to the summit cairn.

The views from the summit are superb, with Loch Leven stretched out below to the west and the southern escarpment of the Ochil Hills disappearing into the distance beyond. West Lomond is the next hill to the east with East Lomond beyond that, and the Lomond Reservoirs nestled beneath them.

Turn left from the cairn towards Loch Leven, dropping to a gate and continuing along the line of an old drystane dyke. Go straight over a crosspaths and along a narrow track to go through another gate and bear right to cross the hillside. Meeting with the outward route, follow it back to the beginning of the walk.

# THE LOMOND HILLS

# The Lomond Reservoirs

**Distance** 10.6km **Time** 3 hours 15
**Terrain** farm roads, hill tracks, minor country roads; some mild ascent and descent **Map** OS Explorer 370
**Access** no public transport to the start

**There is wildlife aplenty on this rewarding circuit around three of the Lomond Hills' six reservoirs.**

The hills are rich in wildlife and there is much to be seen on this walk. Look out for painted lady and small copper butterflies, and for ground-nesting birds such as skylark, snipe and meadow pipit. Stonechat, finches and swallows can be seen on the low open farmland in the summer months, while birds of prey such as kestrel, buzzard and tawny owl hunt for their next meal. You might also spot badger, fox, red squirrel or roe deer.

Beginning in the Holl Reservoir car park at the end of Strathenry Avenue, a single-track road which leaves the A911 west of Leslie, walk back down the road, keeping the reservoir on the left.

Turn right at the crossroads at West Balgothrie, heading along a farm road. Beyond a gate, swing right to climb gently uphill. Turn right at a sign for Harperleas Reservoir, going through two gates to enter a firebreak and climbing gently through the conifers of Harperleas Woodland. Look out for the brick-red common crossbill flitting amongst the trees. Passing briefly through a clearing, Ballo Reservoir can be seen to the east.

Continue straight ahead beyond another gate, climbing to turn left along the edge of the plantation. Drop gently downhill, turning right to walk along a vehicle track beside Harperleas Reservoir. West Lomond, the highest point in Fife, towers over the far side of the reservoir. Turn left to cross the dam, going through a gate on the right at the far end.

Climb to cross a stile and turn right to

# THE LOMOND RESERVOIRS

◀ Harperleas Reservoir and West Lomond

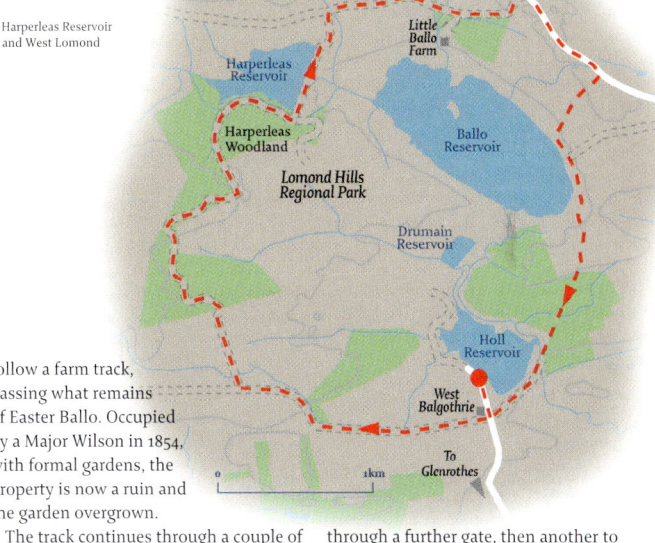

follow a farm track, passing what remains of Easter Ballo. Occupied by a Major Wilson in 1854, with formal gardens, the property is now a ruin and the garden overgrown.

The track continues through a couple of gates. Ignore the road down to Little Ballo Farm, continuing along the track to pass between stone gateposts and turning right onto a minor road through the hills.

Climb gently uphill, turning right to leave the road through an old gate at a sign for Holl Reservoir. Follow a drystane dyke uphill, where the summit has excellent views of all three of the reservoirs. Ballo Reservoir is spread out below, with Harperleas Reservoir in the distance on the right and Holl Reservoir straight ahead beyond Ballo.

Continue downhill, crossing two stiles and going through a gate. Turn left through a further gate, then another to walk along a path near the shore of Ballo Reservoir, parallel to a vehicle track.

Beyond a gate, continue up between two fences and through another gate to cross a field, keeping a drystane dyke on the right. Follow the wall beyond a further gate, climbing over the brow of the hill and dropping down on a path between two drystane dykes.

Beyond another gate, continue downhill to cross an outlet from Holl Reservoir and pass the waterworks. Keep right to climb the hill to the crossroads at West Balgothrie, and turn right to return to the car park.

# Formonthills

**Distance** 3.5km **Time** 1 hour
**Terrain** well-maintained surfaced and unsurfaced paths; some steep ascent and descent **Map** OS Explorer 370
**Access** buses to Pitcairn (Collydean) from Glenrothes, Buckhaven and Leven

Formonthills, which sits on the lower slopes of the Lomond Hills overlooking the northwestern edge of Glenrothes, is a mixture of mature and relatively new woodland. It was created by the Woodland Trust between 1995 and 1997, after they took ownership of the site from Glenrothes Development Corporation. Around 80,000 native trees have been planted, including oak, ash, birch, cherry and Scots pine.

The woodlands are peppered with sculptures, some of which are interactive and may be enjoyed by children. Look out for birds of prey such as buzzard and kestrel, as well as small mammals like rabbits and moles. Roe deer live in the woodland all year round.

The walk begins in Formonthills car park at the top of Benvane Road in Glenrothes. Leave the car park through a gateway at the far end from the road entrance, briefly joining another path before bearing left to walk up an unsurfaced track.

Take the next left, then bear right just before a drainage ditch to enter woodland. These ditches were originally dug to drain the area for farmland. Before that, Formonthills was a hinterland of small lochs, moorland and peatbogs. Take a left through the trees before bearing right to follow another ditch. Go straight over a crosspaths and then turn right beside a metal sculpture of some fungi.

Continue up the hill, swinging right to

# FORMONTHILLS

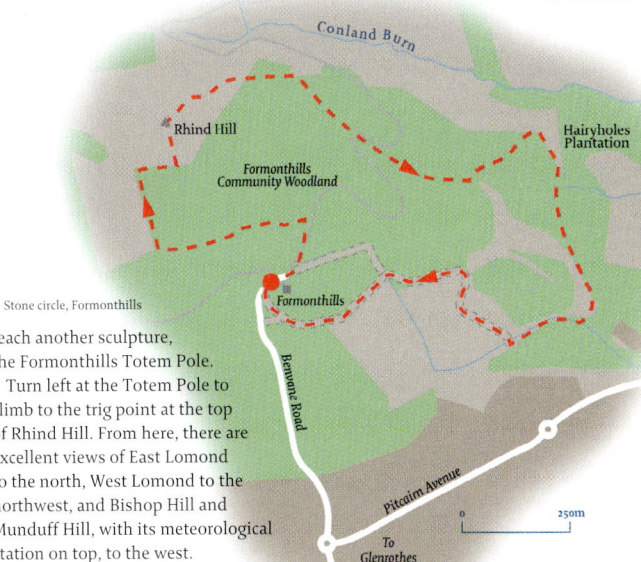

◀ Stone circle, Formonthills

reach another sculpture, the Formonthills Totem Pole.

Turn left at the Totem Pole to climb to the trig point at the top of Rhind Hill. From here, there are excellent views of East Lomond to the north, West Lomond to the northwest, and Bishop Hill and Munduff Hill, with its meteorological station on top, to the west.

Turn right at the trig to amble down a grassy path, bearing right at the bottom of the hill to enter woodland. Turn right at a crosspaths, continuing along the main path and passing through a gap in a drystane dyke. When Formonthills was used as agricultural land, this drystane dyke and others like it marked the boundaries between the fields.

Keep going straight on at a junction, heading across open grassland and over a crosspaths beside two wooden sculptures.

Bear left to drop downhill into a plantation and go straight through and out the other side. Turn right just after leaving the trees and head across the hillside to turn left onto a surfaced path, then right to follow a wall downhill, ignoring the bridge on the left. Local schoolchildren have planted this part of the woodland with native trees, including aspen, rowan, hawthorn, birch, beech and field maple.

Turn right across a bridge over a burn, bearing right to follow the burn before going right again to cross back over and head along a surfaced path over open pasture. There is a stone circle on the hillside to the right, another of the Formonthills sculptures.

Bear left into woodland, continuing straight ahead at the next junction, then right at the fork to leave the woodland and climb back to the start point.

Kinghorn Bay ▶

**Between Burntisland** and Leven, the northern shore of the Firth of Forth becomes quite industrialised. Kirkcaldy, Buckhaven, Methil and Leven are the major settlements, where the economy was historically focused on heavy and traditional industries. But the coast is also interspersed with picturesque villages at Kinghorn, Dysart and East and West Wemyss.

Kirkcaldy is often referred to as the 'Lang Toun' due to its unusually long main street. The town was first mentioned in 1075, when it was granted to the church of Dunfermline by Malcolm III, and it was later given to Dunfermline Abbey by David I. It was only in 1644 that Charles I gave the town its independence from the abbey and made it a royal burgh. Kirkcaldy grew around its port, which became a vital hub for exporting coal, salt and linen during the medieval period. By the 19th century, the town had become known for its production of linoleum, and Kirkcaldy was a world-producer until the mid-1960s.

Kirkcaldy's most famous son was the social philosopher and economist Adam Smith, whose studies of the relentless profiteering of Glasgow's tobacco merchants formulated the ideas which became his magnum opus, *The Wealth of Nations*. First published in 1776, the work still influences economics today.

Further inland, Glenrothes, established as one of Scotland's new towns in the late 1940s, contrasts with Kirkcaldy's historical character. Originally developed to house coal miners, Glenrothes has since grown into an administrative and retail hub for Fife.

# Kirkcaldy and South Fife

**1 Balbirnie and Star Moss** 56
Explore the woodlands around Markinch, returning through the Balbirnie Estate

**2 Kennoway Den** 58
Enjoy a relaxing ramble through a wooded gorge

**3 Silverburn and Letham Glen** 60
Follow coastal and farm tracks north of Leven, returning through an enchanting wooded glen

**4 Coaltown of Balgonie** 62
This tranquil circuit explores the quiet country lanes around Coaltown of Balgonie

**5 East Wemyss to Buckhaven** 64
Explore the caves of East Wemyss before strolling along the Wemyss Private Railway to Buckhaven

**6 Carden Den** 66
This beautiful walk through a deep wooded gorge returns by the site of Scotland's last duel

**7 Ravenscraig Park** 68
An historic castle and picturesque harbour await you on this short circuit

**8 The Mill Dam Path** 70
Leave the formal gardens of Kirkcaldy's Beveridge Park behind for an engaging woodland walk

**9 Seafield and Kinghorn** 72
Traverse the rugged coast between Kirkcaldy and Kinghorn, returning through quiet countryside

**10 Grangehill** 74
Take a hike into the bucolic hinterland above Kinghorn

# Balbirnie and Star Moss

**Distance** 9.1km **Time** 2 hours 45
**Terrain** surfaced and unsurfaced tracks, country roads **Map** OS Explorer 370
**Access** trains to Markinch from Edinburgh, Kirkcaldy, Cupar and Dundee; regular buses to Markinch (High Street) from Leven and Glenrothes

**Follow a causeway across a wooded peat bog before returning through the extensive gardens of Balbirnie House.**

The walk begins on Northall Road in Markinch. Follow the road out of town, passing beneath a railway bridge. Bear right by a cottage to walk up Cuinin Hill ancient roadway, an unsurfaced track thought to have been the route used by Edward I of England when he entered Markinch in 1296.

Turn left over a stone stile to continue towards the summit of Cuinin Hill, going through a gate, descending to cross a road and continuing down the track on the other side. Turn left at the far end to walk down to Star.

Entering the village, turn immediately left towards Broomfold Farm. As you approach the farm, bear right along a vehicle track. Where the track veers left, continue straight ahead to follow a track which leads to a long embankment through the woodland of Star Moss, whose name comes from the Gaelic *stair*, meaning a 'causeway across wetland'. The moss was formerly used for peat cutting but it is now a Site of Special Scientific Interest, supporting diverse habitats such as birchwood, grassland and fen.

Emerging from the trees, head up a wide path, turning left at a crossroads. Just beyond a large house on the left, go straight over another crossroads. Turn left 800m later to continue along another vehicle track through Lochmuir Wood, bearing right at a fork and turning right onto a road which leads through a gate and

◂ Star Moss woodland

out of the woodland.

Cross a railway at a bridge before joining a road, going carefully straight ahead and turning left through a gate on the first corner. Turn right to continue through the woodland, bearing right at a fork to drop down to Balbirnie Stone Circle. Originally erected 125m northwest of here more than 4000 years ago, the circle was moved to its present location in the 1970s to allow the A92 to be widened.

From here, turn left to follow a formal path through the grounds of Balbirnie House. Balbirnie Estate dates from around 1640, when it was acquired by the Balfour family. It remained with the Balfours until 1969, when it was bought by the Glenrothes Development Corporation, who partly remodelled it as a golf course and parkland.

Turn left by the clubhouse to cross the car park and go through the exit at the far end. Turn left at a crosspaths to cross the Back Burn, turning immediately right to continue along the path. Swing right to cross the burn again and go straight ahead up the hill.

At the top, turn left, bearing left again at the next two forks to emerge onto Stobcross Road. Cross over and turn right, looking out for the Stob Cross on the right. The cross is thought to be of Pictish origin but had its ornamentation destroyed during the Reformation.

Turn left onto School Street, turning left again at the bottom of the hill to follow Northall Road back to the beginning of the walk.

# Kennoway Den

**Distance** 8km **Time** 2 hours 15
**Terrain** good surfaced and unsurfaced
tracks; country road **Map** OS Explorer 370
**Access** buses to Windygates (Leven Road)
from Kirkcaldy, Leven and Dundee; trains
from Edinburgh to Cameron Bridge
Railway Station just south of Windygates

This circuit traverses an old railway line before dropping into a picturesque woodland gorge, returning via farm tracks. Part of this route follows a country road with no pavement, and walkers with dogs or children are advised to treat this as an out and back walk through the Den.

From the car park by the roundabout on Leven Road on the edge of Windygates, follow the pavement of the A915 and take the first left, heading along an unsurfaced track to join the former trackbed of the East Fife Central Railway. Originally built in 1898 to transport coal, the line mostly carried seed potatoes and grain. Continue along the old railway, turning left after around 700m. Turn left again onto Sandy Brae, then immediately right into Kennoway Burns. The village's name is derived from the Gaelic *ceann in*, meaning 'place at the head', in reference to its location at the end of Kennoway Den.

Keep straight ahead, then go down wooden steps on the right, signed for Kennoway Den, to follow a wide track along Kennoway Burn. The Den was formed around 13,000 years ago, when meltwater from a glacial sheet surged through, cutting through the soft sandstone. In the 18th and 19th centuries, the water of the Kennoway Burn powered four mills. These are long gone, but the sluices and lades which diverted the water to the mill wheels can still be seen. Today, the only sounds in the Den are from the birds. Look out for grey wagtails, coal tits, great spotted woodpeckers and wrens.

Immediately after swinging across the

# KENNOWAY DEN

◀ Kennoway Burn

burn on an old stone bridge, bear right, climbing steeply uphill to pass a totem pole. Skirt around a vehicle barrier, turning left to return to the burn.

Turn right to continue along the burn, crossing over again to climb steeply out of the Den into open farmland, with a superb view of the Lomond Hills.

At the end of the path, turn left to go carefully along a country road. Ignore the first left, to Newton of Kingsdale Farm, but take the second, heading down a single-track road through a narrow strip of woodland. The road offers excellent views across the Forth to North Berwick. Passing the cottages at Newton Hall, bear left to drop downhill on a farm track, continuing between two fields.

The farm track ends at a bridge over the Markinch Burn, but cross the bridge, climbing uphill on an unsurfaced foot track and swinging sharply left to briefly join a road by some cottages.

Bear right to leave the road at Balcurvie Smallholdings, following an unsurfaced foot track between fields. At a junction, turn left, continuing straight down to turn left onto Main Street. Turn right down a path beyond the first house, going straight down to cross Bankhead Place and continuing down Balcurvie Road.

Turn left onto Milton Road at the bottom of the hill, going straight over the crossroads to arrive back on Leven Road.

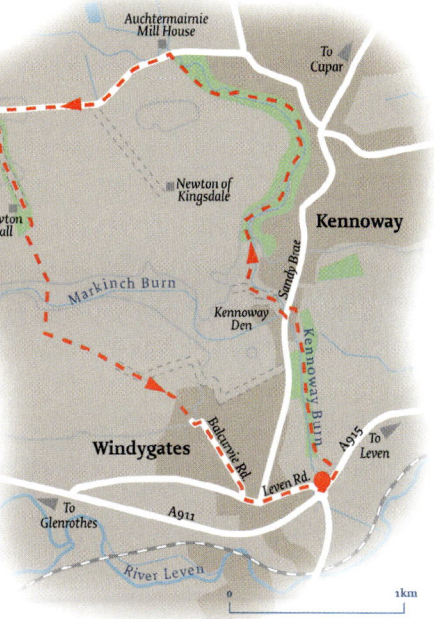

# Silverburn and Letham Glen

**Distance** 7km **Time** 2 hours
**Terrain** good surfaced and unsurfaced paths; mild ascent and descent
**Map** OS Explorer 370 **Access** buses to Leven from Dunfermline, Kirkcaldy, Glenrothes, St Andrews and Edinburgh; trains to Leven from Edinburgh

This circuit follows the coast north of Leven before turning inland to return via a delightful dell.

Beginning on Leven's Promenade, head along the road with the sea on the right. Turn left just before the entrance to Leven Beach Holiday Park, following the Fife Coastal Path around its landward side and continuing along the coast beyond.

Turn left onto a sandy track to cross the golf course. At the far side, turn right through a gate, then left to cross a car park and go along the path at the end.

Pass the buildings of Silverburn Park, continuing straight ahead at a junction to swing around a wildlife pond and turning right to zigzag up the hill. Turn right at the top, then immediately left and right again to go through woodland. Turn left onto another path, following it to turn left onto the entrance road to Silverburn.

Reaching the entrance gateway, cross the main road and turn right, then left at the entrance to Blacketyside Farm. Continue straight along the road, passing the farm, where there is an excellent farm shop and café, and going straight over a crossroads. At the next junction, go along the second of the two roads on the left to reach a road.

Continue straight along the minor road directly opposite. Turn left at the next junction, continuing along a farm track and following the signs to bypass the farm at Coldstream. Further on, bear left, then take a hard left through stone

# SILVERBURN AND LETHAM GLEN

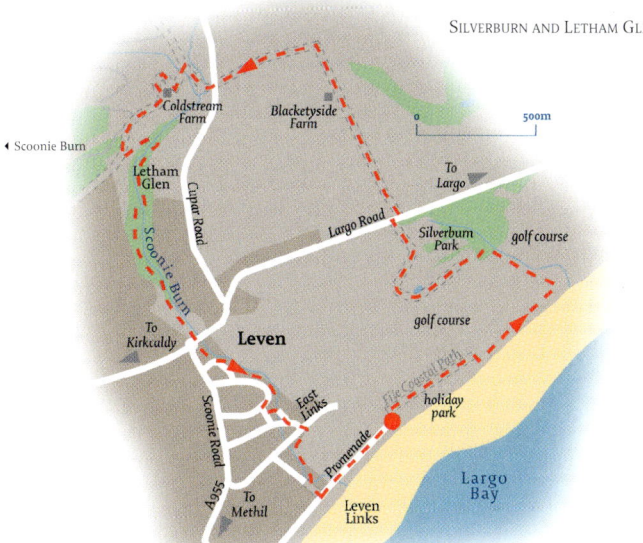

gateposts to go down into Letham Glen, crossing the Scoonie Burn on a bridge above a small waterfall and following the burn downstream through the beautiful wooded gorge.

Letham Glen, originally known as Sillerhole Glen, was feued by the landowner, Mr R Maitland Christie, to Leven Town Council in 1925, for an annual fee of £115, when the council wanted to acquire the land for a public park. That same year, John Letham donated £1000 to the council to be invested to pay for the lease of the glen. The glen was renamed Letham Glen in his honour.

Bear right to cross the burn again, turning left onto a wider path, where the woods give way to the public park. Go through the left of the two gates at the park entrance, crossing the road and continuing along the burn down the path on the other side.

Cross a road and follow the burn to emerge on Scoonie Drive, where you turn right. Keep ahead (left) to shortly go left onto Balmoral Terrace and first left onto a path. Immediately after crossing the burn, turn right down East Links, going left at the bottom and left at another T-junction to remain on East Links.

Turn immediately right, continuing up a grassy trod at the edge of the golf course and swinging right around the back of houses. Turn left to take a formal path back towards the sea, crossing the Scoonie Burn again on the way. Turn left at the next junction to return to the Promenade and the start.

# Coaltown of Balgonie

**Distance** 8.6km **Time** 2 hours 30
**Terrain** farm roads, surfaced tracks; minor ascent **Map** OS Explorer 367 **Access** buses to Coaltown of Balgonie from Glenrothes, Leven and Kirkcaldy

**This relaxing amble along the farm tracks around Coaltown of Balgonie is perfect for lazy summer afternoons.**

In the late 18th century, Coaltown of Balgonie was a mining and weaving village, although Coaltoun is mentioned as part of the barony of Balgonie as far back as 1665. Today, only the A92 separates the village from the new town of Glenrothes.

The route begins at the junction of School Road and Main Street in Coaltown of Balgonie. Facing Main Street from School Road, turn right and head down Main Street. After 350m, turn left by Lady Nina Cottages. Irish-born Lady Helena McDonnell, known as Nina, married local landowner Captain Charles Balfour of Balgonie Castle in 1888. Balfour was a cousin of Arthur Balfour, Prime Minister between 1902 and 1905.

Dodge around a barrier at the end of the road, where the road continues as a foot track between two hedgerows. Turn left at the bottom and continue along a farm track. Skirt around another barrier to arrive at the corner of a minor country road, continuing straight ahead.

Once prevalent here, numbers of grey partridge have declined hugely since the

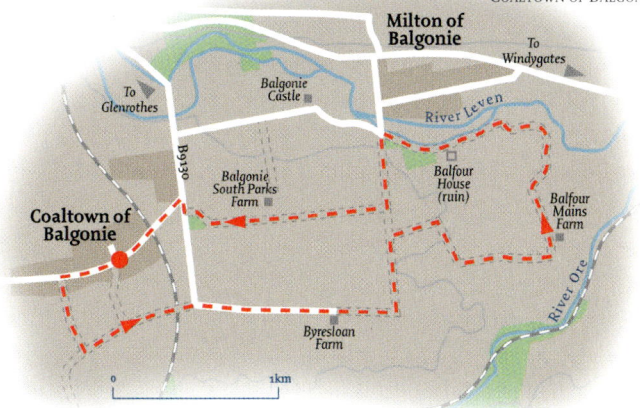

1960s and the fields on the right have been sown specifically to help the species to flourish. Plants such as mustard and chicory provide nectar-rich habitats for insects. These in turn provide food for the birds in summer, while the plant seeds do the same in winter. The plants also provide places to hide from predators and safe spaces to rear young.

Beyond Byresloan Farm, go around a gate and along the lane, turning left at the end, then right at the next junction. The ruins of Balfour House, once a grand Scots Baronial mansion, can be seen to the north.

After passing Balfour Mains Farm, wind down the hill to walk alongside a burn for a little. Entering woodland, turn left through a gate at a junction, then right at a crosspaths just beyond, dropping down to meander along the wooded banks of the River Leven. The track is lined with wild garlic in spring.

Skirt around the boulders at the end of the track, turning left to climb out of the woods. Looking back at the top of the short climb, Balgonie Castle can be seen to the northwest. The castle dates back to at least the 14th century. Its most famous owner was General Sir Alexander Leslie, leader of the Covenanters during the 17th-century wars. He is, allegedly, the subject of the nursery rhyme, 'There Was A Crooked Man'. In 1716, Hanoverian General William Cadogan was using Balgonie Castle as his headquarters for the quelling of Fife, but it was captured by the Jacobites under the command of Rob Roy MacGregor.

Take the next right, continuing along a farm track again. Walk straight ahead at the junction at Balgonie South Parks Farm, skirting around a wooden barrier and continuing along the farm's access road. Turn right at the end of the road, then left to head back along Coaltown of Balgonie's Main Street to the beginning of the walk.

◀ Balgonie Castle

# East Wemyss to Buckhaven

**Distance** 5.8km **Time** 1 hour 45
**Terrain** surfaced and unsurfaced tracks; short but steep ascents and descents
**Map** OS Explorer 367 **Access** buses to Back Dykes, East Wemyss from Leven and West Wemyss

**Explore the caves of East Wemyss before following the former route of a private railway to Buckhaven.**

Beginning in the car park at Back Dykes, East Wemyss, head north along the seafront to the caves. East Wemyss' name derives from the Gaelic *uamh*, meaning 'cave'. The caves are home to several ancient Pictish carvings and guided tours of the interiors can be arranged.

The first is Court Cave, so called because an incognito King James IV is said to have joined the company of gypsies here and enjoyed their hospitality. The next cave is Doo Cave; nesting boxes are carved into the cave walls in this rare example of a medieval cave doocot. The path then curves uphill to approach the ruins of the 14th-century MacDuff's Castle. The Thanes of Fife had a castle here in the 11th century, though it was torched by Edward I of England.

Turn right by the castle to pass Well Cave and return to the shore. Continue along the coast, rounding an outcrop to reach Jonathan's Cave, which contains the largest group of carvings. Return around the outcrop, bearing right to climb steeply through a gully.

Turn right at a junction, joining the former route of the Wemyss and Buckhaven Railway, part of a network of mineral railways built by the Wemyss Estate, known collectively as the Wemyss Private Railway. Opened in 1881, the

# EAST WEMYSS TO BUCKHAVEN

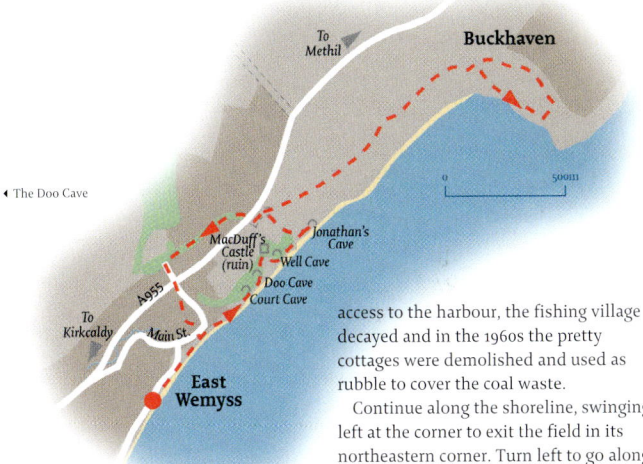

◀ The Doo Cave

railway connected Buckhaven with the main line at Thornton; it closed in 1980. Follow the old line towards Buckhaven.

Bear right immediately beyond a set of steps to pass beneath a wooden archway. At the next right, drop downhill to a large grassy field which was formerly Buckhaven Harbour. In 1831, Buckhaven had the second largest fishing fleet in Scotland. The harbour was constructed in 1838 to accommodate the larger vessels required for deep sea fishing. Tourists arrived by train in droves to enjoy Buckhaven's golden sands and scenic fishing village. But in 1910, in Scotland's worst ever case of coastal destruction, coal waste from the Wellesley Colliery destroyed the shoreline and filled the harbour 6m deep in pit redd. With no access to the harbour, the fishing village decayed and in the 1960s the pretty cottages were demolished and used as rubble to cover the coal waste.

Continue along the shoreline, swinging left at the corner to exit the field in its northeastern corner. Turn left to go along a track, turning right to climb up to another archway.

Turn left and, ignoring the track on the left, follow the fence towards a grassy corner, turning left to follow the railway back towards East Wemyss. On reaching the A955, cross the road and drop down the embankment beyond to continue along the railway.

Descending steps at the end of the track, turn immediately left to curve through the remains of an old railway bridge and cross the A955 again, continuing briefly down East Brae opposite, but quickly turning right to descend through East Wemyss Den. Continue towards the sea at the bottom, crossing Main Street to follow the outward route back to the beginning of the walk.

65

# Carden Den

**Distance** 6.8km **Time** 2 hours
**Terrain** surfaced and unsurfaced tracks
**Map** OS Explorer 367 **Access** trains to Cardenden from Edinburgh; buses to Cardenden from Kirkcaldy and Glenrothes

Lined with tall conifers, the deep atmospheric gorge of Carden Den takes its name from the Pictish *cair*, meaning a 'fortified place'.

The walk begins on Platform 2 of Cardenden Railway Station. The village of Cardenden began in 1848 when the Edinburgh and Northern Railway opened this station at the northern end of Carden Den to serve the local mine workings.

Take the exit path down to the road, continuing up the path directly opposite. Turn off to the right below a railway viaduct down an unsurfaced track. Climbing to join another track, turn right to continue along the surfaced path which leads through Carden Den, following the route of the Den Burn, which runs through the deep wooded gorge.

Approaching the A92, bear left beside a bridge across the burn, soon heading beneath the road, which crosses the gorge on a huge flyover. Bear left, staying on the main path and climbing out of the Den. Skirt around a barrier at the top and turn left onto a wide forest road at the crossroads beyond.

Look out on the right for a monument to the last duel in Scotland, held on 2 August 1826 after George Morgan, manager of the Bank of Scotland in Kirkcaldy, refused a loan to Kirkcaldy linen merchant David Landale. Following an altercation between the two men on Kirkcaldy High Street, involving an umbrella, Landale, despite never having fired a gun, wrote to Morgan, challenging him to a duel. Morgan had been a Lieutenant with the 77th Regiment

◀ Carden Den

of Foot and was confident of winning but when the two men faced each other and shot, it was Morgan who was killed. Landale was subsequently tried for murder in Perth, but was acquitted.

Take the grassy trod directly opposite the monument, swinging to the right and following it along a fence to the scant remains of Carden Tower. A charter of William the Lion from 1170 refers to Carden, and it is likely that the woodland here was a royal hunting forest. In 1482 James IV granted the lands to the Martin family of Midhope, near South Queensferry, who built Carden Tower, a three-storey tower house high above Carden Den. The house was still occupied in 1694, but by 1725 it was in ruins.

Return to the road and continue along it, crossing the A92 by a bridge and bearing right immediately beyond.

Go up the hill, dropping to bear left, then immediately right to enter woodland. Follow a well-defined track, bearing left and then left again through the trees.

At the end of the track, turn left onto Carden Avenue, then left at the end of the road and, just before the playpark, turn left down Cardenbarns Road. After the road swings left, turn right to cross a burn by a narrow bridge.

Follow the path beyond, turning right to drop down steps into Carden Den and then right again to follow the outward route to the beginning of the walk.

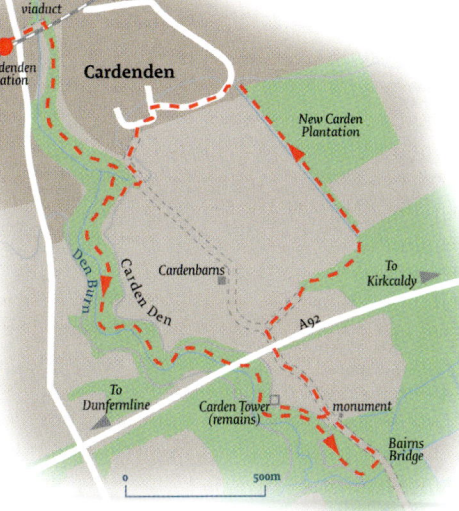

# Ravenscraig Park

**Distance** 3.2km **Time** 1 hour
**Terrain** surfaced tracks; some ascent
**Map** OS Explorer 367 **Access** buses to
Ravenscraig Park from Kirkcaldy
and St Andrews

This short walk, perfect for long summer evenings, visits Kirkcaldy's Ravenscraig Castle before following the Fife Coastal Path to Dysart's historic harbour.

Formerly the grounds of Dysart House, Ravenscraig Park was part of the estate sold by the 5th Earl of Rosslyn to Kirkcaldy linoleum magnate Michael Barker Nairn to pay his gambling debts. Nairn's son gifted it to the people of Kirkcaldy in 1929 and Dysart House became the home to an order of Carmelite nuns.

Beginning in the park's car park, just off Kirkcaldy's Dysart Road, go through the metal archway and turn right to follow the path to Ravenscraig Castle.

Go straight over the crosspaths. The path narrows to disappear behind some modern flats before arriving at the castle. One of the first Scottish castles designed to be defended from and by artillery, work on the castle was begun in 1460 by James II and ownership passed to William Sinclair in 1470. Despite being torched by English raiders in 1547 and damaged by the forces of Oliver Cromwell in 1651, the castle remained in the Sinclair family (later the Earls of Rosslyn) until 1896.

The long flights of steps leading down from the castle to the beach below are said to have inspired John Buchan's classic novel *The Thirty-Nine Steps*. Buchan was brought up in Kirkcaldy and played on the beach as a child.

Returning to the crosspaths, turn right, taking the next right to head downhill into woodland, dropping down steps to reach an old doocot. The pigeons would

◀ Dysart Harbour

have been an important source of food for the castle's occupants. Turn left at the doocot, following the Fife Coastal Path and keeping right at the next junction. A lookout tower, an early 19th-century garden folly and gazebo, sits at the end of an ornate wall.

Keep right at the next fork and right again to emerge through a gateway onto open grassland, with excellent views across the Forth to East Lothian. Turn right at a crosspaths to loop around a wall before going through a tunnel cut through the cliff. The tunnel was hand-cut through the rock to allow ballast from empty ships arriving at Dysart Harbour to be taken by cart to the beach for disposal.

Emerge onto the very picturesque Dysart Harbour, where you can explore the old cobbled dockside. Ships laden with salt, and later coal, left here destined for Europe. Dock gates allowed vessels to load and unload regardless of the state of the tide. Rounding the end of the harbour, turn left to climb up a narrow flight of stone steps. By an exit onto the road, continue up the steps, turning left at the top and continuing up more steps to return to Ravenscraig Park.

Turn right, going straight over a crosspaths and turning left onto a surfaced path. The walled garden on the right once supplied flowers, fruit and vegetables to Dysart House.

At the next crosspaths, turn right, then immediately left to briefly pass through a former arboretum, quickly emerging onto open parkland. Follow the path back to the car park.

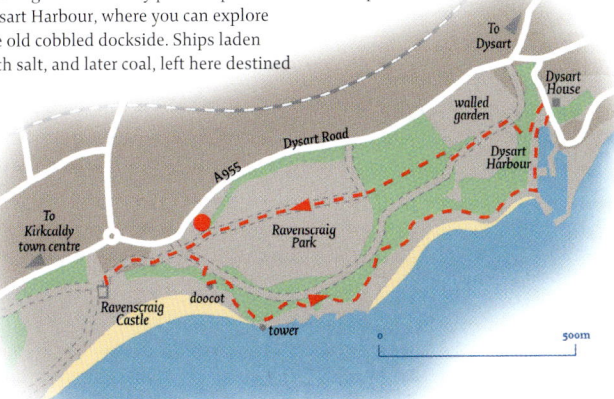

# The Mill Dam Path

**Distance** 4.4km **Time** 1 hour 30
**Terrain** surfaced paths and unsurfaced woodland tracks **Map** OS Explorer 367
**Access** buses to Beveridge Park from Kirkcaldy, Leven and Kelty

**Explore Kirkcaldy's Beveridge Park, before following a forest path along the edge of a drained lake.**

Beveridge Park opened in 1892 after Provost Michael Beveridge left £50,000 in trust to create a park in Kirkcaldy. Beginning at the park's car park, enter the park and turn right. This path forms a circuit around the edge of the park. Between 1948 and 1988, it formed the track of the Kirkcaldy Grand Prix, a major fixture on the motorcycle racing calendar.

Go around the formal rose garden and out the far side, turning left to walk around the boating lake. The first rowing boats on the lake were introduced in 1904. After returning to the main path, turn left at a sign for the Peace Garden to reach a fountain. The beaver at the top is part of the Beveridge family coat-of-arms. Turn right, then right again on the main path, and skirt round a barrier to leave the park.

Turn right onto Southerton Road, turning left at the junction at the far end. Cross the road, and turn right along the road to Kirkcaldy Lawn Tennis Club. Skirt to the right of the clubhouse, following a track around the courts to descend into woodland. Just before a little bridge over a burn, bear left to follow a woodland track through the trees. Raith Lake can be seen through the trees to the right.

Swinging towards Boglily Road, cross over and go through a gateway on the other side. The track shadows the road for a little before climbing away into the

◀ The Mill Dam Path

woods. Bear right to follow a fence downhill, turning left onto another path at the bottom.

This is the Mill Dam Path. The Mill Dam was a 19th-century artificial lake created by building a dam with a weir across the Tiel Burn – the burn to your right. A lade from the dam powered the West Mill. This path, which ran along the edge of the lake, has been popular with walkers for many years. However, the lake was not safe and in 1989 the dam was found to be in breach of new EC regulations and the lake had to be drained.

Reaching a junction by a Fife Core Paths waymarker, turn hard left uphill, almost doubling back on yourself. Bear right at a fork, doubling back again. Keep right at the next fork to follow a pleasant track through the trees.

This is the Wizard's Walk. The 'wizard' was the well-travelled 13th-century mathematician and scholar Sir Michael Scot, who lived at nearby Balwearie Castle. His fascination with alchemy, astrology and the occult gained him a reputation as a great wizard.

Descending to a junction and leaving the woodland, turn right to rejoin Beveridge Park's main path. At a fork beyond the rugby ground, both paths lead back to the car park.

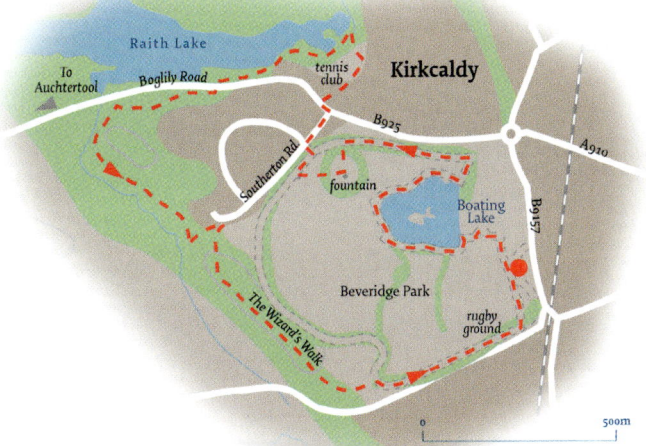

# Seafield and Kinghorn

**Distance** 9.8km **Time** 3 hours
**Terrain** surfaced and unsurfaced tracks, minor roads; mild ascent and descent
**Map** OS Explorer 367 **Access** buses to Kirkcaldy from Dunfermline and Leven

**This route follows Fife's rugged coast from Kirkcaldy to Kinghorn, before returning via a series of minor roads on the hillside above.**

Head south from Kirkcaldy's Seafield Beach car park along the Fife Coastal Path, soon arriving at the ruins of Seafield Tower. The tower was built by the Multrare family around 1542. It passed through various owners, but was abandoned in 1733, after which it fell into disrepair. Skirt around the tower, climbing gradually to follow the railway line, undulating above the shore before dropping dramatically in a couple of switchbacks and continuing south.

Pass between the railway and a caravan site before swinging right to go under the railway, and follow a paved path to reach Kinghorn's Nethergate. Turn left to go under the railway viaduct. Built in 1846 by the Edinburgh and Northern Railway Company, this was part of Fife's first railway. The line connected to the world's first roll-on, roll-off ferry, between Granton and Burntisland, and up to Perth.

Beyond the viaduct, turn immediately right, heading up Harbour Road, and turn right to cross the railway by the station footbridge, which dates from around 1850.

Turn left to climb Station Brae. Cross over the two roads on either side of the war memorial and continue straight ahead up Baliol Street. Turn left past the

# SEAFIELD AND KINGHORN

primary school, turning right onto the golf course at the end of the road, and follow a grassy track up the edge of the course. Meet with the corner of a road and continue up the hill. Drop down some steps, crossing a road and continuing straight ahead along Burnside Path.

Where the path begins to zigzag up the hill, take a left to leave it, passing a pond and rising to meet and cross the B923. Turn left, then bear right to leave the road and pass Kinghorn Loch. The loch is a kettle hole lake, formed when a piece of ice broke off from a retreating glacier during the last ice age.

Just past the Ecology Centre building, keep on round the loch via a short fenced path to an access road, bearing left here and right past a lochside parking area to climb uphill through Craigencalt Farm, turning right at the junction beyond.

Continue on the farm access road past cottages and across the hillside to reach Kissing Trees Lane. Go left, then take the next right, through stone gateposts, to continue along a potholed vehicle track past Banchory Farm. Pass the cottages at Drinkbetween and continue along the farm access road before turning right at the junction to descend between fields on Jawbanes Road and meet with the B9157.

Cross over, turning right to pass beneath the railway bridge, and carry on down towards the sea. Cross back over as soon as you can, continuing down to cross Kinghorn Road and turning right along it, going left down Seafield Road to return to the car park.

◀ Seafield Tower

73

# Grangehill

**Distance** 6.1km **Time** 1 hour 45
**Terrain** surfaced and unsurfaced tracks; mild ascent and descent
**Map** OS Explorer 367 **Access** buses to Kinghorn from Dunfermline, Kirkcaldy and Leven; trains to Kinghorn from Edinburgh and Dundee

**Grangehill rises steeply from the Firth of Forth west of Kinghorn. This easygoing circuit takes an old road over a shoulder of Grangehill before meandering through the countryside above the town.**

Kinghorn, from the Gaelic *ceann gronn*, meaning 'head of the marsh', is a very old settlement. The Scottish court visited Kinghorn's royal castle in the time of the House of Dunkeld. King Alexander III died here in 1286, after falling from his horse near Grangehill, sparking the Wars of Scottish Independence.

The walk begins at the station footbridge on Kinghorn's Harbour Road. Cross the railway line by the footbridge, turning left to climb Station Brae. Cross over the two roads on either side of the war memorial and continue straight ahead up Baliol Street.

Turn left past the primary school and left again onto the golf course at the end of the road. Keep to the left of a line of white posts along the edge of the course. Pass the clubhouse and turn to the right at the car park to go up a stony vehicle track which leads across the golf course. As you climb, views open out across the Firth of Forth to Inchkeith, with Edinburgh beyond.

Leaving the golf course, bear right to stay on the main road, dropping downhill and going through a gate to pass Grangehill Farm. At one time, this was the road from Kinghorn to Binnend, a shale works and now abandoned village a few miles north of Burntisland.

As the road descends, there are views

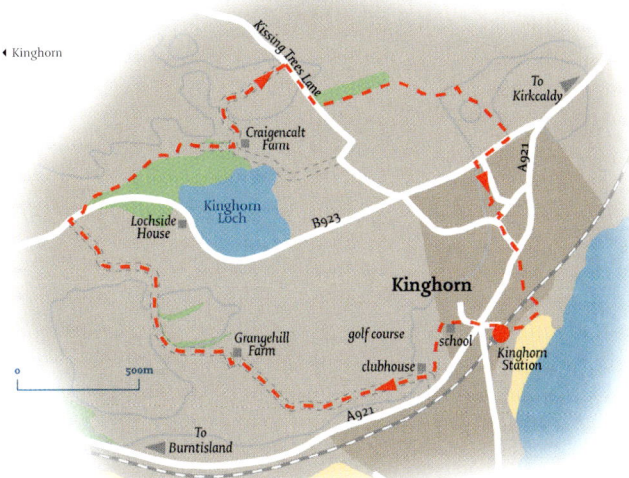

◀ Kinghorn

across Kinghorn Loch. Reaching a gate across the road, go through a small gate at the side and turn right to stroll along the B923. Where the pavement ends, cross over and continue up a track, known as Bramble Lane, signed as the public path to Kinghorn Loch. Ignore the path to Rodanbraes, then bear left, climbing to swing past some allotments.

Go left at the junction immediately before Craigencalt Farm, climbing steeply to go through a gate. Look out for the lade on the right, which drove an 18th-century waterwheel when Craigencalt was a mill. Continue past the cottages along the farm access road, bending right before reaching Kissing Trees Lane at the junction. Turn right, then go left 200m later along an unsurfaced track at the edge of a field, emerging beside a football pitch. Turn right onto a road with houses along one side. Pass Croft an Righ and Orchard Road, then turn left down an unsurfaced track beyond the next house. Follow this track, Templars Walk, to its end, crossing the end of Templars Crescent and continuing downhill before turning right onto Eastgate.

Turn left at the end of the road. Walk down North Overgate, cross St Leonard's Place, go down South Overgate and turn left onto Nethergate. Continue down to the seafront, turning right onto St James Place. Carry on along the waterfront, turning uphill by the sailing club to return to the beginning of the walk.

**In the mid-11th century**, King Malcom III moved his court to Dunfermline and married Margaret of Wessex, sister of Edgar II of England, who had fled to Scotland following the Norman invasion in 1066. The queen, later to become St Margaret, was a very pious woman who founded a ferry service at the narrowest point of the Forth to provide a crossing for pilgrims on the way to St Andrews. The queen's ferry gave its name to the settlements that grew up around the service.

The three great bridges which today cross the Forth at North Queensferry span three centuries. The Forth Bridge, which carries the main railway line north from Edinburgh to Dundee, Aberdeen and Inverness, is a masterpiece of 19th-century civil engineering and has UNESCO World Heritage status. The Forth Road Bridge was the longest suspension bridge in the world when it opened in 1964, but only buses, taxis and motorcycles use it since the opening, in 2017, of the Queensferry Crossing, which carries the M90 north.

Margaret also founded a Benedictine chapel in Dunfermline, which evolved into the magnificent Dunfermline Abbey, the final resting place of seven Scottish kings. She was canonised in 1250.

Further west along the Forth, the saintly connection continues. Culross is reputed to be the birthplace of St Mungo, patron saint of Glasgow, and the burial place of St Serf. Dunfermline's most famous son is Andrew Carnegie, who was born into poverty in the town in 1835. After emigrating to America in 1848, he began working in the cotton industry before establishing the Carnegie Steel Company, which quickly made him one of the world's richest men. During the last years of his life, however, he gave away most of his great fortune to charities, foundations and universities.

# Dunfermline and West Fife

**1 Saline Glen and the Temple** 78
Traverse a deep, wooded ravine, returning via a Victorian observatory

**2 Craigluscar Hill** 80
Enjoy extensive views from the scant remains of two Iron Age hillforts

**3 Balgownie Wood** 82
Walk through ancient woodland, returning along an old railway line

**4 Townhill Country Park** 84
Explore the former site of 19th-century heavy industry, now returned to nature

**5 Valleyfield Woodland Park** 86
A short circuit exploring the former estate of Sir Robert Preston

**6 Preston Island** 88
This landlocked former island was once home to industry but is now a nature reserve

**7 Fordell** 90
One of Scotland's earliest railways leads to a gentle woodland stroll

**8 St Bridget's and the Braefoot Battery** 92
Visit a medieval church and some First World War defences

**9 Aberdour and Silver Sands** 94
Follow the Fife Coastal Path to Burntisland, before climbing to traverse the hillside above Aberdour

# Saline Glen and the Temple

**Distance** 5km **Time** 1 hour 30
**Terrain** unsurfaced woodland and hill tracks **Map** OS Explorer 367 **Access** buses to Saline from Dunfermline

**Explore one of the last remnants of Scotland's Great Forest, before climbing to enjoy the superb views from a Victorian folly.**

Turn right out of the car park at the bottom of Saline's Main Street and walk uphill. After 30m, leave the road to the left, beside an information board, heading down an unsurfaced track into Saline Glen. This woodland dates back to the end of the ice age. Look out for red squirrels playing among native Scottish species such as oak, bird cherry, ash, downy birch, wych elm and hazel.

Stay on the main track, walking parallel to the burn which runs through the glen below, before dropping down to cross over the burn and back again on a couple of wooden bridges. Climb away from the burn, passing beneath a large pipe, before climbing steps up the side of the glen.

Turn left at the top, bearing left again at a fork to undulate through the trees and climbing steadily to walk beside a fence. The fence and path turn sharply right before the track drops down to a clearing. Climb back up to almost meet with the road, but swing left just before reaching it.

Pass some houses and stay on the track

# SALINE GLEN AND THE TEMPLE

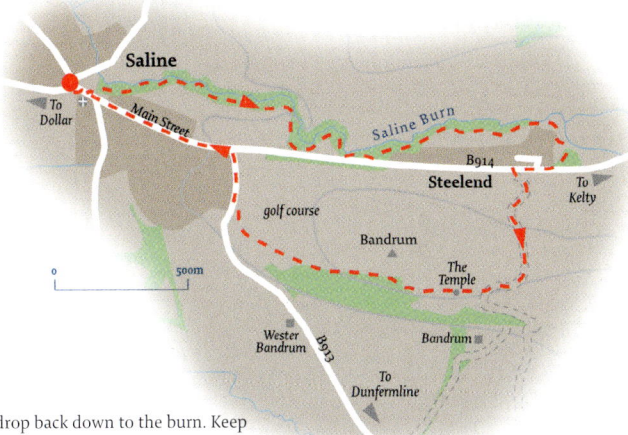

to drop back down to the burn. Keep right at a fork to emerge onto a large playing field, following the perimeter eastwards for 200m before going through a gateway back into the trees.

At a junction, turn right onto a wide track and pass some garages before joining the B914 and turning right. At Midfield Terrace, cross the road to wind gently uphill on a farm track signed for Cowstrandburn. Cresting the hill and beginning to descend, go through a gate and turn immediately right up a small set of steps signed for 'Saline via The Temple'. The unsurfaced track strikes out across the hillside, going through a couple of kissing gates to reach the Bandrum Temple.

The tower commands excellent views across the Firth of Forth to Edinburgh, the three bridges and West Lothian. David Black, who owned the Bandrum Estate, erected a wooden look-out tower here at some point between 1805 and 1813 to commemorate the Battle of Trafalgar. This stone replacement was built in 1845 by the estate's next owner, former sea captain Archibald Hogg, as an observatory. Archibald used it as a summerhouse, but he enjoyed teasing his wife that it was somewhere for him to go after they quarrelled.

Continue across the hillside beyond the temple, going through another couple of kissing gates, before swinging right through a final kissing gate and a metal gate to drop down to a narrow country road. Turn right, following the road down to a junction before turning left to follow Main Street back down to the car park.

◀ Bandrum Temple

# Craigluscar Hill

**Distance** 3.7km **Time** 1 hour 15
**Terrain** unsurfaced hill tracks; steep ascent, mild descent **Map** OS Explorer 367
**Access** no public transport to the start

Despite being only a modest 228m high, Craigluscar Hill has commanding views across the surrounding countryside, which made it a prime location for the two Iron Age forts which were constructed on its twin summits. This walk visits the site of both forts before returning via the rear of the hill.

The walk begins in the car park at the top of Craigluscar Road, beside the two huge water tanks at Glassiebarns. To get to it, follow Carnock Road out of Dunfermline, turning right at the sign for Craigluscar Fishery. Go straight over the crossroads and bear left at the fork.

Leave by a track at the top end of the car park. Go through a gate, following a fence, and on through another gate. Snake uphill through woodland of pine, oak, sycamore and birch. Bear left and then right to walk through an avenue of trees around the hill's western shoulder. There are fine views across to Saline Hill, Easter Cairn and Knock Hill to the north. The Bandrum Temple can be seen on Bandrum Hill to the northwest, with the escarpment of the Ochil Hills stretching into the distance beyond.

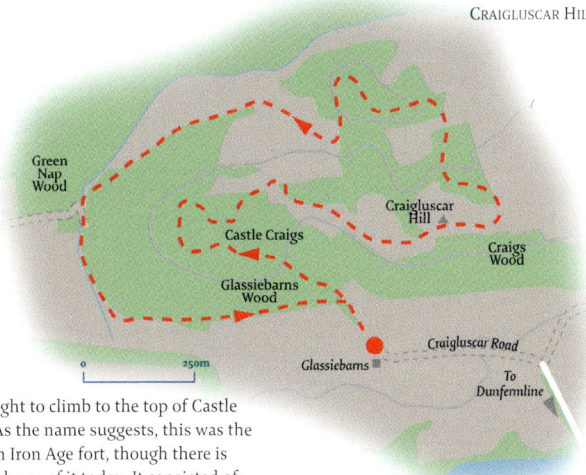

Bear right to climb to the top of Castle Craigs. As the name suggests, this was the site of an Iron Age fort, though there is little evidence of it today. It consisted of three stone ramparts which circled around to the cliff edge on the southeast and west sides. The entrance, to the east, had a wooden bridge. Most of the stonework has been taken away for other purposes over the centuries. The outlook from here takes in Craigluscar's two reservoirs, with Dunfermline beyond those. The three bridges across the Forth at Queensferry lead to Edinburgh, West Lothian and the Pentland Hills.

Continue along the track, dropping to go through an open gateway in a drystane dyke and keep right to follow a wire fence up to the top of Craigluscar Hill. Another Iron Age fort was located here. Like its sibling, it had three ramparts, and an entrance gate supported on four posts. Inside the fort were two large timber roundhouses, which were destroyed by fire. It is thought to date from between 100BC and 100AD.

Drop briefly before climbing to cross a wider summit. Nearing a wire fence by an old drystane dyke, swing downhill to the left, turning left again by a gate to join an unsurfaced vehicle track which leads down through the trees.

At the bottom of the hill, bear right where an ATV track leaves the vehicle track to cross grassy scrub and climbs briefly back into the trees. Reaching a crosspaths, turn right, go across a wide grassy plain and through a gateway in a drystane dyke.

Continue straight over a wide dirt track, swinging left by a burn to go around the western end of the hill and along the edge of Green Nap Wood, before continuing eastwards along the foot of the hill. Arriving back at the gate, turn to the right to go through it and follow the track back to the car park.

◀ Cattle at Glassiebarns

# Balgownie Wood

**Distance** 7.5km **Time** 2 hours 15
**Terrain** woodland tracks; minor roads, surfaced tracks **Map** OS Explorer 367
**Access** no public transport to the start

**Explore this ancient woodland before returning along the route of an old railway line. This land once belonged to the monks of Culross Abbey, who first planted it with oak trees in medieval times. Today, the wood is home to a wide range of wildlife, including red squirrel, roe deer and birds such as crossbill, spotted flycatcher, grasshopper warbler and osprey.**

The walk begins in a small parking area beside the B9037, 1.6km north of its junction with the A985. Go through the gate into the woods and along a surfaced path, bearing right at the sign to Balgownie. Stick to the main path, ignoring the trails that lead off to the right. A footbridge over the Grange Burn takes you out of the woodland to cross a causeway over marshland.

Carry on along the edge of the woodland on the other side of the marshland, crossing a bridge over the Bluther Burn and continuing into sparse silver birch woodland.

Turn left at a junction by a Forestry and Land Scotland sign for Balgownie to follow a wider surfaced vehicle track. Turn left at a waymarker for the West Fife Woodlands Way along a narrow forest track through darker, older woodland, where the forest floor is covered in moss, bracken and dead wood. The oak trees here were regularly coppiced by the monks of Culross Abbey, who stripped them of their bark, which they sold for use in the leather tanning process. Burgh records reference this activity as early as 1654.

The track quickly widens into a long, straight avenue along the southern edge of the woods. Reaching a junction in the

◀ Oak tree in Balgownie Wood

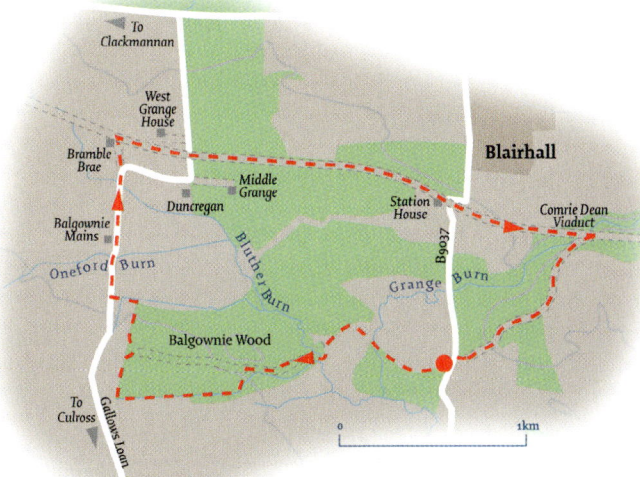

southwestern corner, turn right. Continue northwards along the edge of the woods, turning left at a junction to descend on a rugged track, continuing along the edge of the woods. Turn left, continuing along a single-track road by another car park. The Ochil Hills and Dollar Glen loom on the northern horizon.

Turn right onto a single-track country road known as Gallows Loan, passing Balgownie Mains Farm and crossing an old stone bridge over the Bluther Burn. At a corner just beyond the bridge, turn left up a vehicle track signed for Bramble Brae. Go through a gate on the right, turning right to follow the former trackbed of the Stirling and Dunfermline Railway. This stretch of the line was opened by the Edinburgh and Glasgow Railway in 1850, carrying passengers between Dunfermline and Stirling until 1968. It finally closed to freight traffic in 1982. The line has now been turned into a long-distance walking and cycle route known as the West Fife Way.

Turn right through a gate immediately after crossing the magnificent Comrie Dean Viaduct, some 2.6km along the path. The track offers superb views of the viaduct's eight arches as it crosses the deep gorge of the Grange Burn.

Bear left to follow the wide surfaced track, keeping right at a clearing and dropping down to a farm road. Turn right to return to the B9037 and the start,

# Townhill Country Park

**Distance** 4.3km **Time** 1 hour 15
**Terrain** surfaced and unsurfaced paths; mild ascent and descent
**Map** OS Explorer 367 **Access** buses to Townhill Town Loch from Dunfermline Bus Station

**Explore the industrial heritage of the village of Townhill in this circuit around Town Loch and Townhill Woods.**

There are references to Townhill as far back as 1322, when it was known variously as Monquhir, Moncur or Moncor. In the 18th century, it was renamed Dunfermline Coaltown. Due to its location at the top of a hill leading from Dunfermline, it became Townhill in the early 19th century.

Starting at the Townhill Country Park car park, on the south side of Town Loch, go past the front of the visitor centre, following a sign for the Loch Circular.

Town Loch was once known as Moncur Loch and, at one time, wooden pipes from the loch provided the water supply for Dunfermline Abbey. Today, it is home to the national governing body of water skiing and wakeboarding in Scotland.

The path circles around the loch's western end, crossing over an outlet from the loch. These sluices were put in when the loch was dammed, raising the water level to power Dunfermline's silk mills.

Bear right beyond a bridge, continuing around the loch and entering woodland. At a junction at the northeast corner of the loch, turn left, then bear right to soon join the route of the former Townhill Branch Railway. Townhill Colliery needed to transport its output to the Forth and this

# TOWNHILL COUNTRY PARK

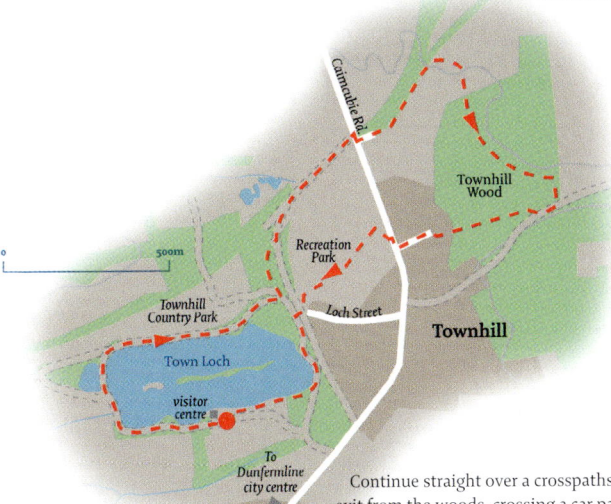

line was opened in 1841 as a horse-drawn wagonway. It was converted to steam in 1880, and extended north to meet the West of Fife Mineral Railway at Lilliehall Junction, which is now a path (Bridle Path) that joins from the left. The line closed in 1976.

On reaching the road, turn right and cross over, following a signpost for Townhill Country Park, and enter the woodland. Pass a sign for the Pugline. This was a branch of the West of Fife Mineral Railway, which led to Muircockhall Colliery.

At a crosspaths, turn right, descending slightly. When you reach a surfaced path, turn right and then bear right again, following a sign for Wilson Street.

Continue straight over a crosspaths to exit from the woods, crossing a car park to follow Wilson Street down to a junction. Cross the main road and turn right, then almost immediately left to enter Townhill Recreation Ground. This was the site of Townhill Colliery, which was opened in 1842 by the Dunfermline Coal Company and closed in 1925. In 1935, the Miners Welfare Fund paid for the grounds to be levelled and turned into a public park. The Townhill Mining Heritage Garden, on the left, gives much fascinating information about the rich industrial heritage of the area.

Turn left to pass a swing park, later forking right along the edge of the Recreation Ground before swinging left to arrive at the end of Loch Street. Turn right to pass beneath a railway bridge, then left to pick up the Loch Circular to return to the start at the visitor centre.

◀ Town Loch

# Valleyfield Woodland Park

**Distance** 2.1km **Time** 45 minutes
**Terrain** formal and informal woodland tracks; mild ascent and descent
**Map** OS Explorer 367 **Access** no public transport to the start

**This short circuit explores woodland created at the turn of the 19th century by the famous gardener, Humphry Repton.**

Sir Robert Preston was a Tory MP between 1784 and 1806, who counted William Pitt the Younger and Sir Walter Scott among his friends. When his brother Charles died in 1800, Preston became the sixth Baronet of Valleyfield. Hiring Humphry Repton, the most sought-after landscape gardener of the time, Preston immediately set about improving his inherited estate.

The estate was sold to the Fife Coal Company in 1907, which stripped the copper from the roof of Preston's magnificent mansion house. The estate was then sold to the Forestry Commission in 1931, who went about replanting the woodlands with Scots pine, larch, spruce, beech and birch, although they stuck to Repton's designs. The derelict mansion was demolished in 1941. The estate was purchased by Dunfermline District Council in 1985 and opened as a public park in 1990.

The walk begins in the Valleyfield Woodland Park car park, which is signed from an unnamed road between the B9037 at Shires Mill and the Clinkum Bank road. Walk downhill through the car park to its far end, turning left to follow a path, ascending gently through the woods.

Bear right to stay on the main path before descending to cross a bridge over a burn. Immediately bear left, climbing wooden steps to briefly reach the edge of the woodland. On the right, the ground

# VALLEYFIELD WOODLAND PARK

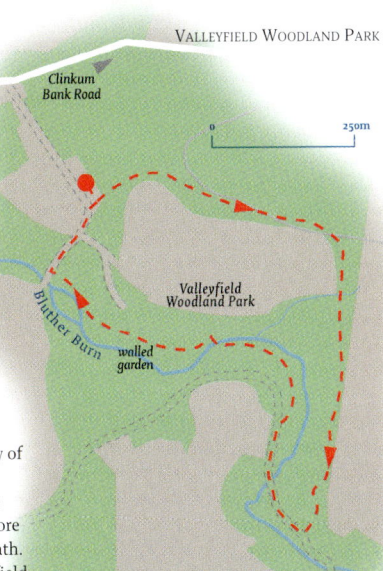

◀ Bridge over the Bluther Burn

drops dramatically away to the valley of the Bluther Burn.

Bear right, dropping down into the valley in a couple of switchbacks before turning right onto a wide surfaced path. In Preston's day, this was the Valleyfield Estate's south drive, constructed by Repton as a scenic carriage drive up the glen. Under his suggestion, the mixed deciduous woodland of the glen was left as nature intended – a decision which was echoed by the Forestry Commission 130 years later.

Cross the Bluther Burn at a bridge which is often so overgrown on either side as to be barely noticeable. Bear right to follow the burn for a little, before turning right to cross a wooden bridge. Bear left just beyond the bridge, then right immediately after to leave the burn.

Amble along the path for a little before taking the next right to climb to the walled garden, a large flat grassy area with a couple of picnic tables. Completed by Repton in 1804, this was a walled south-facing flower garden. Beyond the walls, a ha-ha surrounds the whole garden, which was laid out with fruit trees and ornamental borders. Valleyfield House, Preston's long-gone mansion, once stood at the top of the slope on the other side of the burn from here.

Go back down the hill, turning right to meet up with the burn again and continue on to a junction. The old stone bridge over the burn on the left, another Repton creation, leads to a community orchard and picnic area. Turn right to head back up the hill to the car park.

# Preston Island

**Distance** 8km **Time** 2 hours 15
**Terrain** flat surfaced path, short unsurfaced section which may be avoided by following the return route to the level crossing **Map** OS Explorer 367
**Access** buses to Culross from Alloa and Dunfermline

Preston Island was an artificial island, built around 1800 by Sir Robert Preston to support a complex for producing salt on an industrial scale. The area around the island was infilled by ash slurry from the former Longannet Power Station near Kincardine as part of a land reclamation project, connecting the island to the shore and creating the Torry Bay Nature Reserve. Keep an eye out for oystercatcher, skylark, curlew and merlin.

This circular route is very easy to follow, as it circumnavigates the island with no diversions. Benches are spaced regularly throughout. The walk starts at the Culross West car park. Head east along the shoreside path, which is separated from the sea by a railway line. This is the former Kincardine and Dunfermline Railway, which opened in 1906. Although it closed to passenger services in 1930, the line was used to bring coal from Seafield Colliery in Kirkcaldy to Longannet Power Station until it was decommissioned in 2016.

Where the old pier juts out into the Forth, cross the railway at the level crossing. The pier dates from the 1800s, although the platform at the far end dates from the 15th century. Culross Harbour was filled in when the railway was built, and the disused pier fell into ruin. It was restored by the local community over a number of years and re-opened in 2024.

In the early 1600s, Sir George Bruce built a 5m-tall circular stone tower here, known as The Moat, which was a breakwater for a

◀ Looking back towards Culross

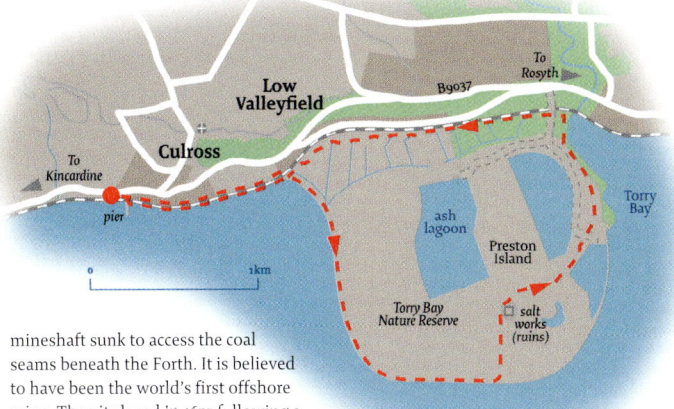

mineshaft sunk to access the coal seams beneath the Forth. It is believed to have been the world's first offshore mine. The pit closed in 1625 following a flood. The remains of the tower can still be seen at low tide.

Go along a narrow unsurfaced track on the other side of the railway until it meets with a surfaced path by a level crossing. Bear right here, at a sign for Preston Island, following the path around the island's southern end, before bearing left to continue inland.

Soon, some ruined buildings come into sight. These are the remains of Preston's saltworks. There were four saltpans in total. The surviving buildings are a row of houses and two pump houses, which kept the waters of the Forth out of three small coalmines. These fuelled the saltpans until 1811, when an explosion killed all of the miners who were underground at the time. Preston suffered substantial financial loss. Salt duties were repealed in 1823, making the production of Scottish salt unprofitable and the saltworks were abandoned by the 1850s.

Continue along the main path, passing a large grassy area with benches looking out across Torry Bay to Low Torry and Torryburn. Keep right to cross a road.

The path soon swings sharply left to head beside the railway line again. Cross the main road into the ash lagoons, continuing beneath a footbridge before bearing left along a pleasant track that winds through trees. Arriving back at the level crossing, cross the railway and follow the path back to the car park.

# Fordell

**Distance** 5.2km **Time** 1 hour 30
**Terrain** woodland tracks and roads
**Map** OS Explorer 367 **Access** trains to
Dalgety Bay from Inverkeithing and
Kirkcaldy; buses from Dunfermline

**One of the earliest examples of Fife's industrial past leads into a peaceful woodland meander.**

Coalmines were established in the lands around Fordell Castle in the 16th century. In 1770, Robert Henderson, 4th Baronet of Fordell, built a wooden wagonway, based on similar horse-drawn wagonways in Tyneside, to carry the coal down to St David's Harbour in what is now Dalgety Bay.

Beginning in the car park at Dalgety Bay Station, return to the road and turn left, walking along the road and turning left again to cross an old stone bridge across the railway.

Taking a hard right on the other side, double back along an unsurfaced track along the edge of a field. Swing left at the end of the field to continue along a straight tree-lined embankment. This was the route of the Fordell wagonway and, later, railway. The line was upgraded and extended over the years, connecting with the Edinburgh, Perth and Dundee Railway near Crossgates in 1850 and converting to steam power in 1867. It finally closed in 1946.

Entering woodland, bear right at a junction, rising to turn left onto a forest road. Keep right to follow the road along the edge of the woods, ignoring the various roads that lead off on the right. The old coalmines were around here.

At a junction, swing left, heading along a road at the northern edge of the woods and ignoring the gated pathway straight ahead where the old trackbed continues northwards.

Before the railway was built, coal from

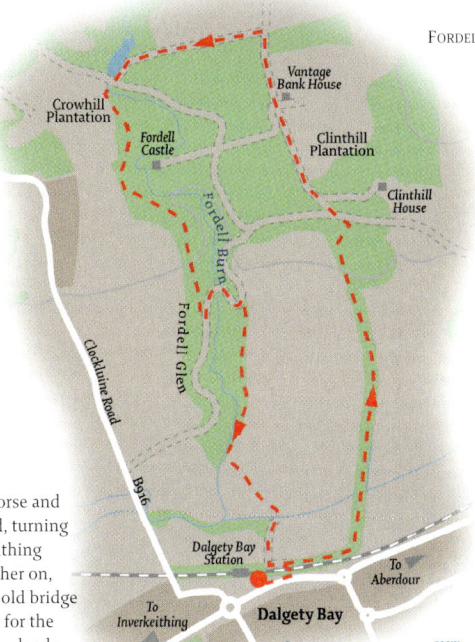

◀ The remains of a bridge

Fordell was taken by horse and pannier down this road, turning south towards Inverkeithing Harbour. A cutting further on, with the remains of an old bridge above it, made it easier for the horses to carry the heavy loads.

The road swings down to the left, passing the gated entrance to Fordell Castle on the left and continuing straight ahead to cross over the Fordell Burn. Just beyond the burn, turn left over a stile into the woods, bearing right just beyond to follow a track through the trees. Drop briefly into the glen of the Fordell Burn before climbing to meet a wall and turning left to follow it.

Take the next left and bear right at the next three forks, staying around 50m from the western edge of the woodland. Reaching a crosspaths, bear left to double back along a wider, more formal woodland track which drops to cross the burn via a 19th-century stone bridge with no parapets. At one time this was the southern driveway of Fordell House, a manor house built in 1721 but demolished in 1963. These woodlands were once the manor's beautiful gardens.

The driveway curls out of the dell. Meeting another path, turn right to meander through the trees on the woodland's eastern edge, reaching and staying by the burn until the track finally veers out of the woods to cut across a grassy field. Leave the field, ambling along a wide farm track to join the outward route back to the railway station.

# St Bridget's and the Braefoot Battery

**Distance** 4.9km **Time** 1 hour 30
**Terrain** surfaced paths, woodland tracks
**Map** OS Explorer 367 **Access** no public transport to the start

Explore a 12th-century church before visiting the remains of a First World War battery hidden in woodland which has grown up around it in the years since.

The old Donibristle Estate, seat of the Earls of Moray, stretched from Inverkeithing to Aberdour. Dalgety Bay, a new town begun in 1965, covers the estate's western end, while the eastern end was an ideal location from which to protect Rosyth Dockyard from enemy attack during the First World War.

The walk begins at the eastern end of Beech Avenue, where there are several parking lay-bys on the road to Braefoot Brae Marine Terminal from the roundabout on the A921 west of Aberdour.

Head down Beech Avenue, joining the Fife Coastal Path and continuing to a junction at the far end. Turn left downhill, continuing straight ahead at the next junction to reach the ruins of St Bridget's Kirk. The kirk dates back to at least 1178, when a papal bull called for the founding of a church at Dalgety. The Augustinian canons of Inchcolm Abbey later began to arrange worship there. It survived the Reformation but in 1641 the minister had to be forcibly removed by soldiers after refusing to leave in protest at the imposition of Episcopalianism by Charles I. Despite alterations in the 17th century, the kirk became unsafe and the roof was lost in 1830. A new church was built 1km away.

Head around the back of the kirk, turning left to follow a narrow footpath above the beach and into woodland. Bear left at the next two forks to climb to a

## St Bridget's and the Braefoot Battery

◀ Braefoot Battery Pier

road. Turn right, then bear left almost immediately to continue along a narrow hedge-lined minor country road.

Where the road bends left, instead turn right through a gate, bearing left immediately beyond to follow a surfaced track through woodland, passing various military buildings which housed the Braefoot Battery during the First World War. A narrow tramway is still visible, leading from one of the buildings, an ammunition store, to the huge gun emplacements behind the buildings. Each gun emplacement housed a BL 9.2-inch Mk IX–X naval gun which could fire a 55kg shell up to 26km.

There are some more military buildings downhill to the right, but instead bear left, passing a pillbox, and carry on to the Braefoot Battery pier. Another pillbox sits beside the track just before the pier. Inchcolm Abbey, whose monks once worshipped at St Bridget's, is just across the bay.

Follow the track back uphill again, passing the two pillboxes before bearing right to follow another woodland track. Turn right at a crosspaths (straight on leads to the top of the gun emplacements). You can see why the battery was situated here; the view takes in the whole of the Firth of Forth, and any approaching enemy ships would have been easy to spot.

Go through a gap in a drystane dyke and turn left to follow the dyke downhill. Go straight across a staggered junction and continue across the fields on a surfaced track. Turn right at the far end to follow the outward route back to the start.

# Aberdour and Silver Sands

**Distance** 9.7km **Time** 3 hours
**Terrain** surfaced and unsurfaced coastal and hill tracks; moderate ascent and descent **Map** OS Explorer 367
**Access** buses to Aberdour from Dunfermline and Kirkcaldy; trains from Inverkeithing and Kirkcaldy

This picturesque circuit follows the Fife Coastal Path between Aberdour and Burntisland before returning via the hills above the villages.

Beginning at Aberdour's Silver Sands car park (fee in summer), follow Dougal's Road, on the right at the far end of the car park, signed for Aberdour Harbour.

Approaching the buildings at the bottom of the hill, turn left, following the Fife Coastal Path up steps and emerging to cross a large grassy plateau.

Drop down steps on the far side to reach two small lighthouses. Known as the Hawkcraig Point Front and Rear Lights, and informally as the Ha' Lighthouses, these mark a deepwater channel in the Forth.

Continue along the road from the lighthouses, turning right by a car park to walk along the edge of Silver Sands Park. Silver Sands is one of Fife's most popular beaches. Turn right by a playpark to cross a bridge. Entering woodland, turn right, following the Fife Coastal Path parallel with the railway line. This eventually goes under the railway, passing a waterfall and continuing to reach a road, keeping straight on to leave it again a few metres later.

Shortly after passing a radio mast on the left, turn left through a narrow stone gateway to leave the Coastal Path, climbing steps before skirting around a

# Aberdour and Silver Sands

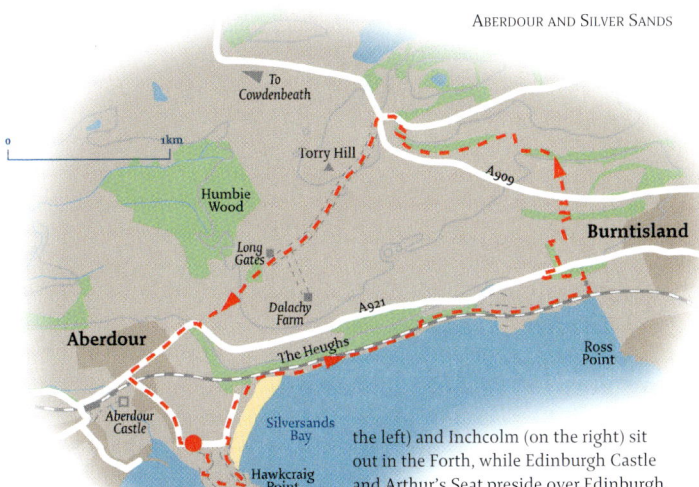

building and swinging left to ascend gently to the A921.

Cross over, turning right to walk along the pavement before turning left through a gateway to continue up a track between the fields, going through another gateway and doubling back on the other side.

Reaching a field, turn left to go around it and drop down to a gate onto the A909. Cross the road and go through a gate opposite, swinging westwards and climbing steeply, aided by occasional steps. This is known locally as the Gorse Cutters Path.

The view across the Forth from this elevated position is far better than that from sea level, with Berwick Law and the Forth Bridges at either end of the panorama. The islands of Inchkeith (on the left) and Inchcolm (on the right) sit out in the Forth, while Edinburgh Castle and Arthur's Seat preside over Edinburgh. The Pentland Hills line the horizon.

Continue along the track, dropping slightly to go through one gate and then another on the right. Climb gently, swinging westwards to walk along a long level track before rising steeply through a couple of switchbacks to turn left onto a single-track road.

Reaching a junction with the A909, cross over to follow a rough single-track road signed as a Right of Way to Aberdour. This is known locally as Kemal's Cut. Where the road swings left, keep straight ahead to pass the cottage at Long Gates. The road degenerates into a narrow footpath which enters woodland and drops gently downhill. Turn left at the bottom, crossing the A921 almost immediately, and turn right to drop down into Aberdour. Follow the road through town, turning left onto Hawkcraig Road to return to the start.

◀ One of the Ha' Lighthouses

# Index

| | |
|---|---|
| Abercrombie | 40 |
| Aberdour | 94 |
| Auchtermuchty Common | 18 |
| Balbirnie | 56 |
| Balgownie Wood | 82 |
| Ballo Reservoir | 50 |
| Balmullo | 14 |
| Bandrum Temple | 78 |
| Birnie Loch | 22 |
| Bishop, The | 48 |
| Boarhills | 32 |
| Braefoot Battery | 92 |
| Buckhaven | 64 |
| Buddo Rock | 32 |
| Burntisland | 94 |
| Cambo | 34 |
| Cardenden | 66 |
| Ceres | 24 |
| Coaltown of Balgonie | 62 |
| Craigluscar Hill | 80 |
| Craigrothie | 24 |
| Craigtoun Country Park | 28 |
| Crail | 36 |
| Culross | 88 |
| Dalgety Bay | 90, 92 |
| Dysart Harbour | 68 |
| Earlsferry | 38 |
| East Lomond | 46 |
| East Wemyss | 64 |
| Elie | 38 |
| Fife Ness | 36 |
| Fordell Glen | 90 |
| Formonthills | 52 |
| Gaddon Loch | 22 |
| Hill of Tarvit | 24 |
| Kennoway | 58 |
| Kilconquhar | 38 |
| Kinghorn | 72, 74 |
| Kingsbarns | 34 |
| Kirkcaldy | 70 |
| Kittock's Den | 32 |
| Letham Glen | 60 |
| Leuchars | 16 |
| Leven | 60 |
| Lindores Loch | 18 |
| Lucklaw Hill | 14 |
| Markinch | 56 |
| Milton of Balgonie | 62 |
| Morton Lochs | 12 |
| Newport-on-Tay | 8 |
| Pittenweem | 40 |
| Preston Island | 88 |
| Ravenscraig Park | 68 |
| Rock and Spindle, The | 30 |
| St Andrews | 28, 30 |
| St Bridget's Kirk | 92 |
| St Michael's Wood | 16 |
| St Monans | 40 |
| Saline | 78 |
| Scotlandwell | 48 |
| Scotscraig | 8 |
| Seafield | 72 |
| Silverburn | 60 |
| Star Moss | 56 |
| Tayport | 10 |
| Tentsmuir Forest | 10, 12 |
| Townhill Country Park | 84 |
| Valleyfield Wood | 86 |
| West Lomond | 44 |
| Windygates | 58 |